CLOCKS

CLOCKS

JOHN
HUNTER

MAGNA BOO

Published by Magna Books
Magna Road
Wigston
Leicester LE18 4ZH

Produced by Bison Books Ltd
Kimbolton House
117A Fulham Road
London SW3 6RL

ISBN 1-85422-397-6

Printed in Hong Kong

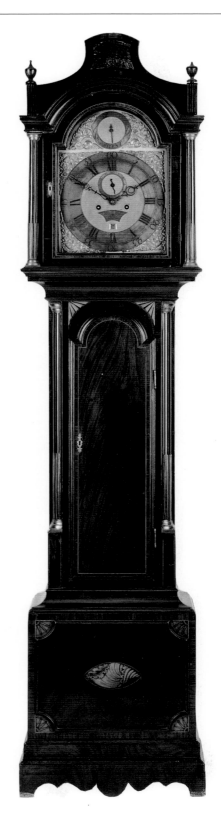

c.1880.
Daniel de St
nventional
musical

th

c.1790,

CONTENTS

Introduction

THERE ARE two essential differences between clocks and most other types of collectable antique and it is these differences which make the study of old clocks – or 'horology', as it is properly known – the fascinating and rewarding pastime that it is for many thousands of people throughout the world today.

The first is that as well as being attractive pieces of furniture in their own right, clocks are machines, ticking away quietly but relentlessly on the mantelpiece or in a corner of the room. This gives an illusion of life, something not possessed by other furnishings. The second is that most old clocks are actually signed by their makers, usually with a place-name and occasionally even with the date of manufacture. Details such as these give the owners a starting point from which they can often progress to finding out much about the life and times of the person who constructed the clock.

The enthusiastic clock owner may look up horological reference books to find out about the history of a particular clockmaker. Failing that, local parish records may be consulted for details of when the maker was born, to whom he was married, how many children he had baptized, when he died and so on. Old trade directories often held by local libraries are another rich source of information on clockmakers of the past. Yet another starting point might be the records of trade associations such as the Worshipful Company of Clockmakers, the London trade guild for clockmakers in the heyday of mechanical horology.

Regardless of where he or she starts, the enthusiastic collector and researcher will glean any scraps of information he can find about a particular clockmaker, or clockmaking family, building them up into a useful body of knowledge about the person or persons concerned.

Many such clock enthusiasts, starting with a single clock and a single maker, have amassed impressive collections of fine antique specimens; many more have marshaled the information gathered over the years and published it in the form of a book about clockmakers from a given area.

This present book makes no attempt to give details of the life histories of more than one or two of the most important and influential clockmakers of the past. It summarizes the evolution of the mechanical clock from the crude ecclesiastical timekeepers of fourteenth century Europe to the sophisticated and complicated mechanical clocks and wristwatches still being manufactured in Switzerland and elsewhere today. It also discusses the major domestic clock types which have been developed over the past three centuries and shows where they fit in the rich tapestry of mechanical horology.

ABOVE
Gilt carriage clock by Detouch of Paris.

RIGHT
Mahogany English workshop regulator dating from the Regency period. These clocks display hours, minutes and seconds on separate dials.

LEFT
Round-dialled Regency bracket clock in mahogany and ebonised case by Roskell of Liverpool.

CHAPTER 1

The Early Days

OBSESSED AS we now are with the measurement of time in its infinite precision, it is difficult to understand the very different relevance of time and time measurement to early man. In prehistory, time was measured by the calendar rather than the clock: the season was more important than the second, the month more important than the minute. While time today is used for keeping appointments, catching trains, measuring athletic performance, its use to early man was in calculating when best to sow the crops, when to hold a religious festival, when to expect a solar eclipse and so on. Those who knew how to predict important natural events were the high priests – the shamans – of prehistoric societies, where wisdom and knowledge were inseparable from religious authority.

Early man had nothing like the need for the precision timekeeping that our sophisticated and complex lifestyle necessitates. The movement of a shadow round a wooden rod stuck in the sand provided timekeeping accuracy more than adequate for the needs of primitive societies. Even as late as the eighteenth century, some church clocks were still being made with only an hour hand, and many domestic timekeepers of the seventeenth century were accurate only to the nearest 'half quarter' (seven-and-a-half minutes).

As these primitive societies progressed, however, accurate timekeeping became increasingly important. The sophisticated civilizations of the Ancient Egyptians and Greeks required a higher degree of precision in timekeeping than the tribes from which they had evolved. Meetings had to be arranged, events had to be scheduled – and timekeeping was provided in a variety of ways. The wooden rod stuck in the sand was superseded by the rigidly constructed and accurately delineated sundial, which has diversified and developed over the centuries into the many types to be found throughout the world today.

The movement of water from one container to another was also used for its timekeeping properties in the water clock or 'clepsydra'. Time would be measured by the fall-ing level of water in a container as it dripped slowly out of a hole in the base. Another method involved floating a bowl with a tiny hole in the bottom on top of a container of water. The unit of time here was the time it took the bowl to fill up and sink.

The problem with water clocks, however, was that they could freeze: they would not work when the temperature fell below the freezing point of water – and so sand came to be used in place of water, the time unit here being the time taken for a quantity of sand to flow from one container through a constricted opening into another container placed below it. These sand clocks have evolved into the familiar 'egg timer' still used today.

The first clocks which had what we now recognize as an 'escapement' – albeit a very primitive one – was the astronomical water clock built towards the end of the eleventh century by the Chinese scientist and diplomat Su Sung, on the instruction of the boy emperor Chao Hsu and his ministers. Within two years, Su Sung had built a working model of a clock of unprecedented complexity. Six years later the clock itself was ready. At that time, Su Sung's clock must have been one of the wonders of the civilized world. It occupied a large building, weighed several tons and was used to chart the movements of the sun, moon and stars. Much of the construction was of wood, the metal parts being of cast bronze.

The problem with earlier water clocks was the fact that water flows out of a container at an uneven rate – fast when the tank is full, progressively slower as the tank empties. In Su Sung's clock, the water which drove the mechanism was stored in a tank which was kept at a constant level. As it flowed out, the water filled one of a number of scoops mounted round the perimeter of a large water wheel. It was only when the scoop was full that it was able to descend and the wheel moved round. When this happened a series of levers ensured that the next scoop on the wheel was brought to a halt just below the supply of water from the tank – and the whole process started again. This type of cyclical start-stop action has, with very few exceptions, been a prominent feature of

Stonehenge near Salisbury, England. This great stone circle is thought by some to be a giant astronomical clock or sundial for establishing the times of solar and stellar events such as eclipses.

Portable sundial from the late seventeenth century by Johann Willebrand of Augsburg, Germany.

LEFT
Reconstruction of the water wheel
from Su Sung's great
astronomical clock built in China
in the eleventh century.

RIGHT
Detail of a tower clock
movement. The 'foliot' on top of
the movement swings first in one
direction, then the other. With
each swing the 'pallets' below
allow the escape wheel to move
round by one tooth.

FAR RIGHT
Islamic astrolabes such as this
were used by Arabs to measure
the positions and movements of
stars and planets. This allowed
them to calculate time and
latitude.

BELOW RIGHT
A group of sixteenth century
sundials, probably from Florence,
Italy.

clock and watch escapements in the years since, and indeed Su Sung's clock is regarded by many as a link between the early water clocks and the first true mechanical clocks, which it is thought to have surpassed in terms of accuracy and reliability.

The first weight-driven mechanical clocks are thought to have appeared in Italy around the turn of the twelfth century, and these wonderful new devices gradually spread to abbeys, monasteries, churches, cathedrals and other ecclesiastical buildings throughout continental Europe. There are a number of reasons for the 'church connection'. These early clocks – which we would regard today as being crude in the extreme – were at the forefront of technological advancement in the fourteenth century. Ecclesiastical authorities, still the custodians of knowledge and wisdom, were the first to appreciate the significance of this great development. Also, the ecclesiastical day was divided into seven 'canonical hours' – Nocturns (or Matins), Prime, Terce, Sext, Nones, Vespers

and Compline – and was strictly regulated. No other area of medieval society required timekeeping of such precision, and this did not change until the massive sociological upheavals brought about by the Industrial Revolution.

The movements of these early clocks – as, indeed, of later clocks and watches – can be divided into three parts: a drum or 'barrel' which converted the movement of a slowly falling weight into a circular motion; a series or 'train' of gears or 'wheels' which reduced the power of the falling weight to a more manageable level and culminating in a wheel known as the 'escape wheel'; and a mechanism which allowed the power to dissipate or 'escape' in regular bursts, and in so doing gave the clock its timekeeping properties. This last is known as the 'escapement' and it in turn must receive a push – or 'impulse' – with each burst of power from the escape wheel in order to keep the whole process going.

Escapements of these early clocks used a verge and

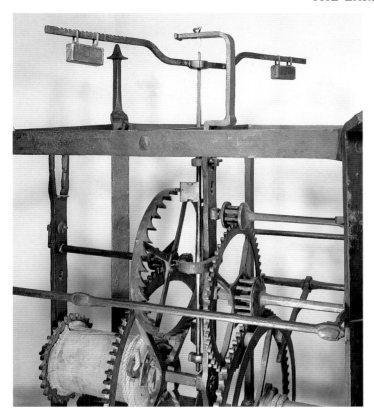

foliot arrangement. The accuracy of this type of escapement was very much dependent on the power delivered to the escape wheel which, because of the crude construction of these clocks, could vary greatly as the wheels slowly turned. At their best, these early clocks were able to keep time to within perhaps quarter of an hour per day, and were by today's exacting standards highly unreliable.

By the fourteenth century, knowledge of the new clocks and their mechanisms had spread as far as England. Richard of Wallingford, Abbott of St Albans from 1327 until his death in 1336, published details of his 'Great Clock' in the manuscript *Tractacus Horologii Astronominici*. It is perhaps significant that Richard's account gives details of only the parts of the mechanism which governed the movements of the sun, moon and planets: the reader was assumed to be conversant already with the workings of a clock. Richard's clock was not finished until many years after his death and unfortunately it has not survived.

The earliest surviving church clocks in England were built for the cathedrals of Salisbury in Wiltshire and Wells in Somerset. The church accounts at Salisbury for 1386,

for example, record the building of a house for the keeper of the clock, while the accounts at Wells in 1392/3 have an entry relating to the clock keeper's wages. The movement of the Wells clock can now be seen in the Science Museum, London; that of the Salisbury clock is on display in a transept of the cathedral. These clocks are thought to have been made by the same person. Records also exist of a clock built for the tower of Norwich Cathedral in the 1320s, but the clock itself has not survived.

The earliest clocks were simple devices without outside dial and hands. The movements were in 'birdcage' form, consisting of a series of vertical strips of wrought iron held together top and bottom by horizontal bars. The wheels were mounted on axles or 'arbors' which were pivoted at either end on the vertical strips. The movements were mounted in the tower or 'turret' of the church or cathedral – to allow an adequate drop for the weights – and were attended by a clock keeper who, besides winding the clock up, regulating it and performing simple maintenance tasks, struck a bell in the tower when the clock showed the appropriate time. The word 'clock' is in fact derived from the Latin *clocca*, a bell.

Gradually, through the decades which followed, the clock towers housing 'turret' clocks acquired a dial and hands to allow the time to be displayed to the public at large. At first a single hour hand only was used, though as the verge was replaced by the more accurate anchor escapement, their accuracy improved and they were given a minute hand.

The anchor escapement – invented towards the end of the seventeenth century – was pendulum controlled and was more accurate and easier to regulate than the verge. With its introduction, the timekeeping of public clocks improved greatly. The discovery of cast iron led to another development in turret clock technology towards the end of the eighteenth century – the 'four-poster'

frame. Like the birdcage which it superseded, the four-poster was an upright rectangular framework with, as the name suggests, substantial posts at the four corners, these being held together top and bottom by horizontal strips of cast iron. Vertical strips of the same material were bolted to the back and front of the movement and it was these which carried the wheel pivots.

In the years which followed, clocks began to move out of purely ecclesiastical establishments into other public buildings, such as town halls, local government buildings and (eventually) large department stores. It was just such a clock in just such a public building which, in the 1850s, was to set the trend for public clocks into the next century, a clock which incorporated two significant

LEFT
Movement of the Wells Cathedral clock, one of the earliest surviving British turret clocks.

RIGHT
Dial of the astronomical clock at Hampton Court Palace, England, made around 1540 by Nicholas Oursain.

ABOVE
Movement of a longcase clock by
Joseph Knibb, showing the anchor
escapement which was responsible
for a quantum leap in the
accuracy of mechanical clocks in
the seventeenth century.

LEFT
One of the earliest known spring-
driven pendulum clocks made by
Salomon Coster of the Hague.

RIGHT
The tower which houses the Great
Clock of Westminster, known
affectionately – if incorrectly – as
'Big Ben'. Considerable damage
was done to both the clock and
the inside of the tower when the
movement cracked on 5 August
1976.

advances in turret clock technology.

This was the Great Clock of Westminster, now often referred to – incorrectly – as 'Big Ben', a name which properly belongs to the massive bell which hangs above the movement and on which the hours are struck. Incidentally, the bell is generally assumed to have been named after Sir Benjamin Hall, Chief Commissioner of Works at the time the present Palace of Westminster was being built. Recent thinking has it, however, that it was actually named after a notorious heavyweight prizefighter of the day, Benjamin 'Big Ben' Caunt, whose name was often applied to anything that was the heaviest of its kind.

The original Houses of Parliament had burned down in 1834 and in the following year a competition was organized for the design of the new building. The competition was won by the architect Charles Barry, whose plans included an imposing clock tower. Barry knew little of clocks and consequently, after consultation with Sir G B Airy, then the Astronomer Royal, three makers were asked to submit tenders for the job – B L Vulliamy, E J Dent and Whitehurst of Derby. The tenders were duly submitted in 1846 and 1847, but were not acted upon until 1851, when Edmund Beckett Denison (later Baron Grimthorpe) was asked by Airy to advise on the construction of the clock. Denison, a lawyer by profession and a noted amateur horologist with an interest in turret clocks and bells, did not like any of the designs submitted and set about designing the new clock himself.

The movement which finally went into construction – designed by Denison and manufactured by E J Dent – incorporated Denison's new double three-legged gravity escapement. In this escapement the pendulum receives its impulse – the extra 'push' needed to keep it swinging – by the action of a gravity arm falling against it. Whereas in most escapements the impulse comes direct from the escape wheel – and is thus at the mercy of variations in power transmitted down the wheel train – here the escape wheel has the effect of raising an arm which then falls under the action of gravity and impulses the pendulum. As the force of gravity is constant, impulse to the pendulum is constant, with the result that the large force needed to drive several sets of hands in inclement weather – rain, wind, snow, ice – does not adversely affect the timekeeping of the clock. The Great Clock of Westminster was one of the most accurate public clocks of its day.

The Westminster clock also set the style for turret clocks to come, by using the flat-bed movement – a type of movement which appears to have been introduced by Grimthorpe from France – where the wheels are mounted in a 'flat' cast-iron framework, more robust and rugged than the birdcage and the four-poster, and with no equivalent in domestic clocks. Despite its more rugged construction – and despite the fact that many birdcage movements have operated successfully for centuries – a crack which appeared in the chiming mechanism of the Westminster clock (and possibly other cracks) caused the clock movement to fail and break up at 3.45am on 5 August 1976, resulting in extensive damage to both the movement and the inside of the clock tower. After much research into the cause of the failure, the clock was repaired and set in motion again on 4 May 1977.

Following the original installation of the Great Clock of Westminster in the 1850s, and as a direct result of its spectacular success, flat-bed turret clock movements with Grimthorpe's gravity escapement proliferated throughout the civilized world and the vast majority of turret clock movements manufactured in the intervening years incorporated either or both of these innovations.

CHAPTER 2

The Lantern

THE EARLIEST domestic timekeepers, like the turret clocks from which they were derived, were made entirely of iron. These were the 'chamber' or 'Gothic' clocks of central Europe, examples of which can still be examined in museums in several European countries. These clocks in turn are the direct predecessors of the 'lantern' clock, which appeared in England around 1600. Early examples of the lantern clock were also made largely of iron, though brass was soon adopted by its makers, probably because it was easier to work, more attractive in appearance, less prone to corrosion and, above all, it was available in quantity.

By 1620 the lantern clock style was fully developed, though it was to evolve still further as the years progressed. Many of these early lanterns were made by Huguenot refugees, Protestants who fled to England from France to escape religious persecution. In fact the word 'lantern' as used to describe these clocks may have a French origin. Although it is generally attributed to a fancied resemblance of these clocks to medieval lanterns, some authorities believe that it is a corruption of 'laiton', the French word for brass. In contemporary documents, lantern clocks are often referred to as 'brass' or 'house' clocks. Other names for this type of clock include 'Cromwellian', 'bedpost' and 'birdcage'.

Early lantern clocks were not made by clockmakers as such. This was a new trade which had not yet developed sufficiently to have gained recognition in its own right, so a variety of craftsmen in allied trades, mainly blacksmiths, but also locksmiths, whitesmiths and others, turned their talents to clockmaking. Official recognition of the craft of clockmaking in England did not come until 1631, when Charles I granted a charter of incorporation to a group of London clockmakers petitioning to set up the Worshipful Company of Clockmakers.

The lantern clock was the first truly English clock style to be produced in any numbers. It did not achieve the same degree of popularity elsewhere, though some very fine lantern clocks were made in France and, to a lesser extent, Italy. Continental lanterns are markedly different

LEFT
Lantern clock dating from around the middle of the seventeenth
century. The narrow chapter ring is typical of early lanterns.

ABOVE
Verge escapement lantern clock by Benjamin Hill of London, who died
in 1670. Right: Winged lantern – the short pendulum used in this type
of clock hangs between the time train in front and the striking – or in
this case alarm – train behind, swinging out into the triangular
protrusions on either side of the clock.

in style to their English counterparts.

In England, the lantern clock enjoyed a long period of popularity: lanterns were still being made well after the introduction of the weight-driven grandfather or 'long-case' clock and the spring-driven 'table' or 'bracket' clock. In the first decades of the eighteenth century, for example, the same clockmaker might be making clocks of all three kinds. One possible reason for this is that the lantern was simpler in construction than its wooden-cased competitors. Another possibility is that the lantern was relatively portable: it could be carried from room to room, from town to town.

Whatever the reason for its continued popularity, lanterns were still being made – especially in the provinces, which were less fashion conscious than London and its environs – well into the eighteenth century, when it was

finally ousted by the longcase. Even in mid-Victorian times, 250 years after their introduction, the lantern clock maintained a degree of popularity. Clocks in the form of lanterns can still be found with key-wound spring-driven movements. Some of these were made, and others converted by Victorian clockmakers, further demonstrating the enduring popularity of this type of clock.

The earliest known lantern clocks were made around 1600, 50 or 60 years before the invention of pendulum-controlled timekeepers by the Dutch scientist Christiaan Huygens, and the construction of the first pendulum clocks by Salomon Coster in the Hague. These early lanterns used a verge escapement controlled by a balance wheel without a spring and were very inaccurate. Soon after the pendulum was introduced into England by Ahasuerus Fromanteel and his son John, it was adopted

by lantern clock makers and quickly became a standard feature; it was much more accurate than the balance wheels of the day. Lantern clocks with their original balance wheels are extremely rare today, the vast majority having been converted to pendulum control. An experienced clock repairer can tell where this has been done by the style of the clock, the color of the brass, the presence of unused holes in the movement and so on.

The next spur to further progress in horological technology was the invention of the 'anchor' or 'recoil' escapement which gradually superseded the verge escapement in the decades following its introduction in the final quarter of the seventeenth century. The anchor escapement together with the new 39 inch-long 'Royal' pendulum – which 'beat' seconds (that is, took one second to swing from one extreme to the other) – in-

troduced a new degree of reliability and accuracy into mechanical timekeeping.

Though most lantern clocks extant today were made with verge escapements and short pendulums, many of these in later years had the verge escapement removed and replaced with an anchor escapement and long pendulum. A few were originally built that way.

Lantern clocks which have been converted – whether from balance wheel to verge or verge to anchor – raise an important issue among clock restorers today. Should they return the clock to its original condition or accept the original conversion as a legitimate part of the clock's history and let it stand? Is it better to restore the original escapement or is this further vandalism? Is there any point in removing parts which may already be 250 years old and replacing them with parts which are brand new?

This is the dilemma of restoration versus conservation and will probably be with us for many years to come.

As has already been mentioned, early lantern clocks, with crudely made verge escapements, were inaccurate and unreliable by today's exacting standards. A loss or gain of a quarter of an hour per day was normal and lantern clocks did not require – and did not have – a minute hand. The hour hand alone could show the time with sufficient accuracy, which it did on a chapter ring, the inner band of which was marked with quarter-hour divisions. Early lantern clocks which do have minute hands and 'motionwork' – the 12:1 gearing just behind the dial which runs the minute hand – are thus more than likely to have been converted at a later stage.

In these early days, the lantern clock was often the only clock in a household. It would be hung in the hall or by the stairs, high enough for a fall of weights which would allow the clock to run for a full 12 hours, and in a position which would allow the striking – and alarm, if fitted – to be heard throughout the house. Some lantern clocks were built to stand on a wooden bracket attached to the wall – others had an arrangement known as a 'hook and spike', where a hook attached to the back of the clock hangs on a projection from the wall and two spikes lower down hold it steady. Lantern clocks almost always had striking. Some had alarm. A few had both. Nowadays, with electric lighting and luminous dials, and with clocks cheap enough to have one in every room of a house, striking may seem unnecessary – as indeed it is. But when the lantern clock was devised, striking ensured that a

LEFT
Eighteenth century lantern clock with square dial and alarm by Cartwright of London.

RIGHT
Lantern clock by the great London clockmaker Thomas Tompion.

FAR RIGHT
Eighteenth century lantern clock by George Tyler of London. While most lantern clocks have a single hour hand, this also has a minute hand. The bell is missing from the top of the clock. The presence of winding squares again indicates that this clock has at some stage been converted from weight to spring drive.

wakeful householder could know what time it was even in the dead of night.

Early lanterns, like the continental Gothic clocks from which they were derived, clearly show their origins in the turret clocks of the day. In plain view they are more or less square, rising up like the towers of the churches in which turret clocks were housed. The clock is supported on four turned brass feet. The movements of these clocks also show a strong resemblance to those of turret clocks. There are brass plates top and bottom, held together by posts at the corners. The wheels are mounted in metal strips – almost always of brass – running between the top and bottom plates. The striking train is behind the going train, rather than beside it as in later plate-movement clocks. To either side of the movement are brass doors. Sitting on top of the movement is the balance wheel – if

this is the form of regulation used – and above that the bell on which the hours are struck. Brass frets are mounted on the front and both sides of the lantern clocks to hide the space between the top of the movement and the bell. The whole clock is finished off above the bell with a turned brass decoration or 'finial', with matching finials at the corners.

As this style of clock evolved, a number of variants appeared; one of the most appealing in visual terms was the style now known as the 'winged' lantern. Here the pendulum hung behind the going train but in front of the striking train – ie between the two, rather than at the back. The movement was specially built to make this possible, with the going and striking trains running in separate 'cages' and special slots cut in the side doors to allow for the swing of the pendulum.

LEFT
Lantern clock, c.1700, by John Drury of London. The spike projecting from the rear of the clock helps to hold the clock steady against the wall.

RIGHT
Silver and gilt metal miniature Dutch lantern clock bearing the name 'Fromanteel'.

ABOVE
Very rare English brass carillon lantern clock, c.1665, with a revolving automaton of wooden figures above the dial.

obscuring the movement from the front view. The sheep's head was contemporaneous with the development of lanterns with full arched dials, not dissimilar in shape to the arched dials of longcase clocks and usually signed by the maker in a boss in the arch. Arched dial lanterns, which outlived the sheep's head in terms of popularity, were precursors of the hooded wall clock, the entire movement of which was enclosed in a wooden case, only the dial and hands remaining visible.

The miniature lantern – approximately half the size of the normal lanterns and fitted with alarm as standard in the same way that conventional lanterns were fitted with strike – are generally thought to have been used as an early type of traveling alarm. Travelers could ensure that they awoke in time to have breakfast before the stagecoach left. These clocks are thought to have been supplied complete with wooden carrying cases, though very few of these cases have survived to the present day.

Dating lantern clocks can be a difficult and risky business and only experienced clock dealers and clock

The 'wings' from which this type of clock takes its name were triangular brass extensions on the sides of the clock covering the slots cut in the side doors. These extensions, glass at the front, brass elsewhere and with a special brass fret on the top, allow the pendulum to be seen as it swings to and fro. However, not all clocks with the pendulum between the trains had wings – in some such clocks the pendulum simply swung unimpeded out on either side of the movements. These are often thought – wrongly – to have had their wings removed at a later date. Winged lantern clocks which still possess their original wings are very rare indeed today.

Another variant of the traditional lantern clock is the 'sheep's head', which first appeared around the beginning of the eighteenth century and became popular a few decades later. Here the chapter ring extends well beyond the clock frame, giving the clock a fancied resemblance to the head of a sheep or ram, complete with horns, and

FAR LEFT
'Sheep's head' lantern clock, c.1720. These clocks, with the dial projecting well beyond the case, were thought to resemble the heads of horned sheep. The simplicity of the dial center engraving on this clock shows that it was made by a Quaker.

LEFT
Arch dial lantern clock dating from the middle of the eighteenth century.

ABOVE
Movement of an early eighteenth century lantern clock showing its anchor escapement.

restorers can do it with any accuracy. Later makers often copied earlier styles and provincial makers often lagged behind their counterparts in the more fashionable southeast of England. This problem is compounded by the fact that lantern clocks were often the subject of later alteration, from balance wheel to pendulum, verge to anchor – and, in more modern times, back again. Another popular alteration which may hinder dating is the addition of motionwork to allow the fitting of a minute hand. It re-

quires great expertise and experience to know when such alterations have taken place.

There are, however, some general guidelines which can help the less experienced collector to put a date to a lantern. For example, while early lantern clocks are often signed by the maker in the center of the dial – inside the chapter ring – later models are often signed on the chapter ring itself. Another useful guideline is that early lanterns normally have narrow chapter rings, small enough to fit between the top and bottom plates of the movement. As the style progressed the chapter ring grew in overall diameter and became wider. Also, while the engraving in the dial centers of early lantern clocks is often of a geometric and repetitive form, later clocks normally feature a flowing arrangement of scrolls and foliage. Yet

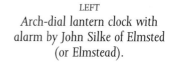

LEFT
Arch-dial lantern clock with alarm by John Silke of Elmsted (or Elmstead).

RIGHT
Lantern clock by the well-known Nicholas Coxeter of London who died in 1679.

26

another useful date indicator is that early lanterns had two weights – one for the going train and one for strike – and normally ran for only 12 hours. Later clocks had a single weight with a pulley arrangement that allowed both trains to be run from a single weight and the going train to run for a full 24 hours.

While these few guidelines will not make a lantern clock dating expert out of anyone – something which can only be achieved immersing oneself for years in the subject – they may give the horological newcomer a very rough idea of the age of a lantern clock he may be looking at.

CHAPTER 3

Clocks in Long Cases

IF THE lantern clock was the first truly English clock type, the grandfather or 'longcase' is the type most often associated with the heyday of British horology. Its stately grandeur is at home beneath the high cornices of imposing country houses. Its slow majestic tick brings back echoes of a time when life was lived at a more leisurely pace. And in fact it was an English longcase clock which inspired the American songwriter Henry Clay Work to immortalize this type of clock – too tall, indeed, for the shelf – in his popular song 'My Grandfather's Clock'.

Despite this almost automatic association with Britain, floor-standing clocks in tall cases actually appeared in countries throughout Europe at around the same time – in Italy, France, Germany, and Holland – and in later years were to appear in other countries, notably the United States and the island of Bornholm, off the Danish coast. It was in Britain, however, that this style of clock reached its fullest flowering and where it was produced in its greatest numbers and diversity.

The British longcase clock is the true and direct descendant of the lantern clock. In fact, to the casual and uninformed observer the longcase looks much like a hooded wall clock to which a body or 'trunk' has been added, allowing it to stand on the floor. In England the first longcase clocks appeared shortly after the Restoration of the monarchy in 1660, a time when the enforced austerity of Cromwell's puritanical Commonwealth was being relaxed and the English people were just beginning to demand more elaborate and flamboyant furnishings.

It may appear that there is a connection between the introduction of the long pendulum and the introduction of the long case – that the longcase was made specifically to cater for needs of movements with pendulums just over 39 inches in length – but this was not the case. The first longcase clocks were made before the invention (by Knibb, Clement or whoever) of the anchor escapement and the introduction of the long or 'Royal' pendulum in about 1670. The first longcase clocks had verge escapements and short bob pendulums.

The evolution of the movements of these early long-cases took place along two separate lines. On the one hand the English lantern clock movement was used as the basis of 30-hour longcase clocks with 'birdcage' movements. This line of development was to die out relatively quickly in all but a few English counties. The second line used 'plate' movements similar to those which had been developed for spring-driven 'table' clocks on the European mainland, but converted to weight drive for longcase clocks. Both 30-hour and eight-day longcase clocks were made with plate movements, and this style of clock was developed by clockmakers throughout Britain into an immense variety of individual styles over the next two and a half centuries. This type of movement, as we shall see in the next chapter, was also the direct precursor of another, peculiarly British, type of clock – the 'bracket' clock.

The movements of early 30-hour birdcage longcase clocks are very similar to those of the lantern clocks from which they were evolving. As the name suggests, the wheels were mounted in a cage-like structure, with the striking train behind the going train rather than side-by-side, as in plate movement clocks. The 'cage' itself was similar to that of a lantern, with a brass plate top and bottom, four pillars or 'posts' at the corners, and brass straps running between the plates to hold the wheel pivots. In fact, birdcage longcases exist which are little more than lantern clock movements mounted in grandfather clock cases.

The plate movement was a different proposition altogether. This was constructed with brass plates back and front, held together by four or five – or sometimes six – pillars. The wheels were mounted with their pivots running in the plates, and the two trains of wheels, if the clock had striking, were side by side – the striking train usually being to the left, and going train to the right, when viewed from the front.

It is often wrongly assumed that plate movement longcase clocks evolved from 30-hour birdcage clocks and that the latter are necessarily earlier than the former. This is not so: both types appeared at around the same time.

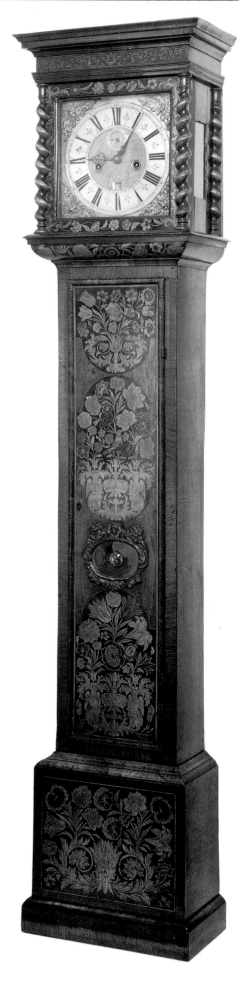

RIGHT
Single-handed longcase clock by William
Flint of Charing, c.1760.

LEFT
Month-going marquetry longcase by Edward
Speakman of London.

The case of the longcase clock consists of three sections – the hood, the trunk and the base. The hood is the top section which goes around the movement and at the front of which is a glass door through which the dial is viewed. This section is usually slid off the trunk to gain access to the movement. The trunk is the part of clock within which the pendulum swings, and it stands on top of the base which is slightly wider and stands directly on the floor. The movement is mounted on a 'seatboard' at the top of the trunk.

While 30-hour longcase clocks, both of the birdcage and plate movement types, use the same form of weight drive as the lantern, where one weight drives both going and striking, and the clock is 'wound' by pulling down the free end of the chain or rope, eight-day longcases have separate weights for each train and these must be wound separately by a key or a crank through holes in the front of the dial. There are no winding holes in the normal 30-hour dial. However, because eight-day clocks were more complex – and so much more expensive and prestigious – than their 30-hour counterparts, clockmakers would often drill winding holes in the dials of 30-hour clocks to make them look like eight-day models. A quick look inside the trunk to see how many weights there are – one for 30-hour, two for eight-day – will allow

RIGHT
Charles II month-going longcase clock by Thomas Tompion of London.

ABOVE
Dial of 'sidereal' longcase regulator by Thomas Tompion and his nephew Edward Banger. Sidereal or 'star' time is slightly out of step with the 'mean' time which is measured by the vast majority of clocks.

FAR RIGHT
Early longcase clock by Joseph Knibb. The cases of early langcase clocks were often ebonised or blackened and they commonly had 'roof-top' or 'architectural' pediments.

even the novice to spot the difference.

As far as dating is concerned, some useful guidelines can be given which will help the novice find the general date of a longcase clock. That said, the browser must remember that many longcases have been extensively altered over the past three centuries. Dials have been swapped, hands exchanged and movements altered in a variety of ways. The most extreme example of this is the making of 'marriages'. In horological terms, a marriage is a clock made up of parts of different clocks – the movement of one clock, for example, the case of another, the dial of a third, the hands of a fourth and so on, all of widely differing periods and styles. These clocks are generally of little value, and putting a date to them is an impossible and pointless exercise.

Early longcase clocks with verge escapements are very distinctive indeed. For a start, they are much smaller than later examples, usually a maximum of six and a half feet high. They always have square brass dials – the 'break-arch' dial was a much later development, as was the white or painted dial. In keeping with case, the dial too is small, only eight or nine inches square, compared with the 11 inch dials which appeared around 1690 or the 12 inch dials of later clocks. The dial of an early longcase clock would have a very narrow chapter ring, while the spandrels (brass castings mounted in the dial corners) would be of an early style such as the so-called 'cherub's head'. The hands would be very simple in style and the maker would have had his name engraved along the bottom of the dial rather than on the chapter ring, as became the fashion later. Some early clocks had a single hand.

The cases of these early longcases are slim and very plain in style, lacking the elaborate mouldings, inlays, marquetry, lacquering and even carving of later examples. These cases, reflecting perhaps some of the austerity of Cromwellian England, were often ebonised – stained black and polished to resemble more expensive ebony. The hood would have an architectural pediment – a shallow triangle in the style of Greek temples – with a column on either side of the dial, these being embellished top and bottom with brass decorations.

One of the first longcase clock developments, as we have seen, was the incorporation of the anchor escapement and its associated long pendulum, an arrangement which quickly took over completely from the verge and bob pendulum in longcase clocks. Incidentally, the fact that this pendulum 'beat' seconds – that is, took a second to swing from one side to the other – meant that the normal 30-tooth escape wheel took a minute to revolve once and thus made seconds indication a simple matter of extending the escape wheel arbor through the dial and mounting a seconds hand on the end of it. Because of the position of the escape wheel, the seconds dial was normally just below the figure 'XII' in the dial center.

Another important consequence of the use of the anchor escapement was that case trunks had to become wider to accommodate the swing of the long pendulum,

and in order to keep the same proportions the hood and dial had to become larger and the whole case taller. Around the same time as the introduction of the long pendulum, the 'lenticle' came into fashion. This is a small oval glass window in the trunk at the same level as the pendulum bob. It allows the pendulum to be seen in motion and remained popular for half a century.

During this period, 1675 to 1725, the oak cases of longcase clocks were normally veneered with more attractive woods – tulipwood, olivewood, walnut and so on – and were often decorated with marquetry or parquetry, a form of decoration in which veneers are a jigsaw puzzle of different-colored pieces of wood, the whole making a geometric pattern (parquetry) or stylized picture (marquetry), the latter often using motifs such as birds, flowers and scrolls.

Shortly after the introduction of the anchor escapement, around 1670, the architectural hood gave way to the flat-topped hood which, as the name suggests, gave the clock a flat squared-off shape at the top which echoed the shape of the bottom. The top was finished off at the front and sides with straight horizontal mouldings. This was quickly superseded before the turn of the century by the 'cushion top', where the hood was built up with a series of mouldings to resemble a cushion. It is important to point out here that the dates given for these developments are the dates when they are thought to have occurred in London. Provincial clockmakers normally lagged behind their London counterparts in the adoption of fashionable trends.

One of the next major developments in the design of

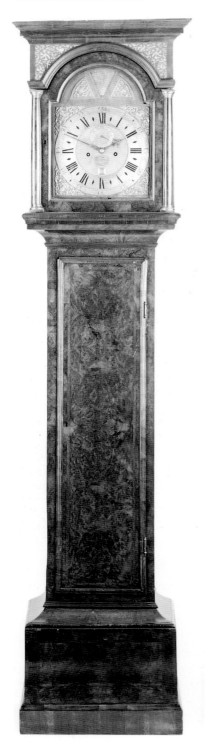

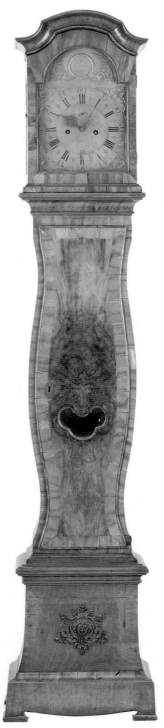

ABOVE
An eighteenth century walnut longcase made by Thomas Finch in London.

ABOVE
The highly unusual shape of this seventeenth century walnut longcase shows that not all longcases conformed to contemporary conventions.

ABOVE
A cushion-topped longcase by Thomas Tompion of London with a lenticle in the trunk door.

ABOVE
An eighteenth century Dutch walnut longcase or 'staande klok'. Note the shaped base, typical of Dutch longcases.

RIGHT
The intricate and detailed face of a Queen Anne longcase.

LEFT
North of England longcases were often in wider, more imposing cases. This George III example is signed 'Finney, Liverpool'.

longcase clocks was the introduction of the break-arch dial around 1710. Here the dial, while still basically square in shape, has an arch at the top which breaks out of the square. This appears to have been introduced by one of the most famous English clockmakers, Thomas Tompion, whose clocks now command extremely high prices on the international market. From soon after its introduction, the dial arch became a common feature of longcase clocks. In some early arched dial clocks, the arch is shallow and might contain only a subsidiary dial and hand which allowed the strike to be silenced. Over the years which followed the dial arch was used for a whole variety of functions, including automata connected to the escape wheel, astronomical and tidal indicators and so on. Some of these indicators performed an important function. Tidal-work, for example, allowed fenland residents to predict the flooding of coastal flatlands.

Moon-work was particularly popular. This showed how much of the moon was going to be visible on any particular night and allowed the householder to take into account the amount of moonlight likely to be available when planning his nocturnal movements. Moon-work was available in a variety of forms, most commonly as a

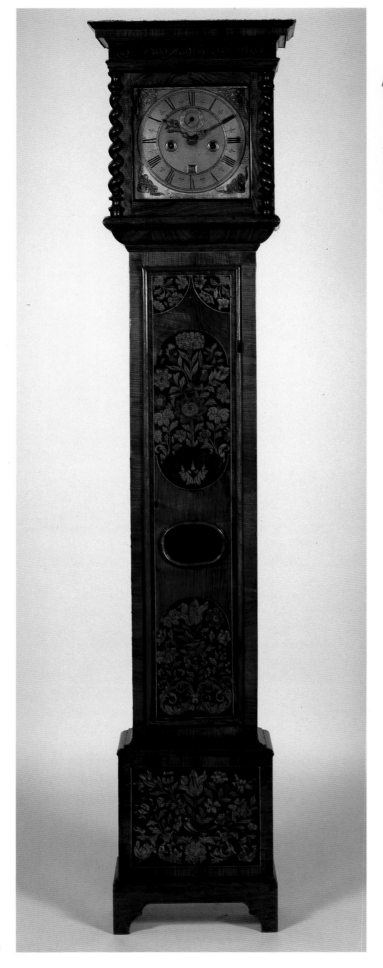

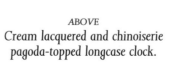

ABOVE
Cream lacquered and chinoiserie
pagoda-topped longcase clock.

ABOVE
Pagoda-topped month-going
longcase clock in a walnut case.

LEFT
This longcase, with its elegant
marquetry case, dates from the
closing years of the seventeenth
century.

two dimensional painting which revolved to show the moon waxing and waning. Other dials had a three dimensional spherical 'moon' which revolved on a vertical axis one side being painted black to indicate the new moon, the other white to indicate the full moon. As it revolved, all states of the moon could be seen.

The introduction of the arched dial also gave rise to a number of different styles of longcase pediment. These include the broken pediment, similar to the early architectural pediment but with the apex of the triangle cut away and replaced with a small urn (beginning in the 1730s); the swan-neck, where each side of the pediment consisted of a matching wooden scroll (beginning in the 1730s); and the so-called 'pagoda top' or 'hollow' pediment, where the sides of the pediment rose in a concave fashion and the very top was convex (1740s). As with lantern clocks, the tops of longcases were often finished off with finials, one at each corner and one in the center.

One of the most important developments in longcase clocks was the adoption of the 'white' or 'painted' dial, which first occurred around 1770 and was soon to become an accepted part of the longcase clock. Prior to this, longcase clock dials had been made of brass, with chapter rings being 'silvered', having had a coating of silver applied chemically. Painted dials, on the other hand, were made in one piece, the front of which was painted white and then painted on top of that with the chapter ring, the maker's name and a variety of decorations.

Until recently, painted dial longcase clocks had been treated as being very much the poor relation of the brass-dialled longcase, often being chopped up for firewood – despite evidence which suggests that early painted dials were actually prestige clocks, and more expensive than their brass dial counterparts. Fortunately, this has now changed and painted dial clocks are changing hands for substantial sums.

Though the arched dial had come into being as early as 1710 and was in common usage by London clockmakers a couple of decades later, the square dial lived on for some time, particularly in the provinces. As a result of this, white dial clocks exist with both square and arched dials.

The dials of early white longcases mimic the dials of brass dial clocks. The corners are painted with patterns

RIGHT
A 12-inch white dial longcase by Cohen of Redruth. Note the figured veneers to the trunk door and base.

ABOVE RIGHT
The arch dial of the Cohen clock shows phases of the moon and high water at Hoyle.

resembling spandrels, often using gold paint. The dial arch might contain simply the name of the clockmaker and the town in which he worked or, like many brass dial clocks, moon-work – painted in much the same way that it was often painted on brass-dial clocks. Perhaps the commonest use of the dial arch was for a realistic painting, often using as its theme a popular issue of the day. As the style progressed, white dials became more flamboyant and colorful. Gradually natural objects – plants, animals, shells and so on – came to replace the formal spandrel-like corner decorations and the dial-arch painting became larger and more vivid.

In its fullest flowering, the white dial was a thing of great beauty, almost an object of art in its own right. Now the corners might have any of a whole variety of popular motifs – such as the Four Seasons, one in each corner, or the Four Continents – or anything that took the fancy of the clockmaker or his customer. The painting in the dial arch would fill all of the space available to it and would be executed in a highly professional manner. By now the dial painting has become a very prominent feature of the clock. The functional dial area is proportionately less than on earlier clocks and the corner decorations join up with one another.

It is important to point out here that, just as the clockmaker did not make the cases of his clocks, he did not make the dial. Brass dials were made by professional and (normally) highly skilled engravers. White dials were made by professional dial painters, this trade being centered on Birmingham.

One important difference between brass dial and white dial longcase clocks, however, is that while the brass dial was made with a particular movement in mind, the white dial was made in such a way that it could be fitted to many different longcase clock movements. The dial makers did this by fitting the dial with a structure known as a 'falseplate'. This was a metal plate which was attached by posts to the rear of the dial. The falseplate could be drilled where necessary to take the posts by which it was attached to the movement.

Longcase clocks also became popular in America, the original American longcase clocks – or 'tall' cased clocks as they are known in the United States – being made by British makers who emigrated across the Atlantic. They established themselves as clockmakers in what was then a British colony; one Abel Cottey is recorded as having worked originally in Crediton, Devon, but emigrated in 1682 to Philadelphia. Early American longcase clocks thus bear a very strong resemblance to their contemporary British counterparts, with similar proportions, similar brass movements, similar dial engraving and so on.

Many of the parts used to construct these clocks – dials, hands, even entire movements in some cases – were actually imported from Britain. This was an expensive and somewhat chancey business, however, and clocks made using imported parts were inevitably more expensive than home-produced clocks. As the years passed

ABOVE
A Victorian white dial longcase in the provincial style by one of the Garratt clockmaking family of Peterborough.

LEFT
A provincial 'cottage' longcase clock with square white dial by Jos. and Wm. Thristle of Stogursy, Somerset.

ABOVE
A Victorian brass-dial mahogany longcase clock. The 'rocking ship' automaton in the dial arch rocks from side to side as the pendulum swings.

RIGHT
A mid-eighteenth century brass-faced longcase.

a generation of clockmakers appeared who had been born, brought up and trained in America, men who had no ties with the Old Country and were thus not hidebound by British fashions and traditions, men like Eli Terry, who introduced mass-production techniques into clockmaking, and his workmen Thomas and Hoadley to whom Terry later sold his factory. It was these clockmakers, and others like them, who began to develop clocks which were more truly American in style, culminating in the 'shelf' clock, the clock which typefies American horology in the way the longcase does British horology.

One overriding factor in the development of American clocks was shortage of brass. This alloy – of which the typical British longcase movement contains several pounds – was in very short supply in eighteenth century America, and American clockmakers had to turn to other materials, notably wood. American longcase clocks do exist which have brass movements – just as British longcases exist which have wooden movements – but these are the exception rather than the rule. They were made

for wealthy people who could easily afford the added expense.

The typical American tall-cased clock, which was made in both 30-hour and eight-day versions, has a chunky wooden movement. The plates are of wood, as are the wheels, pinions, levers and so on. The clock will typically have a painted arched dial. In the early days, dials were often imported, already painted, from Britain. These are impossible to distinguish from the dials of contemporary British longcases, though as the years passed American dial painters developed their own distinctive styles. Some American tall cased clock dials are actually made of paper pasted on to a wooden back-board, again saving on the amount of metal used in the construction of the clock.

The cases also developed their own stylistic individuality. They had similar proportions to British cases though the base was often taller. They carried a minimum of brass decoration – even the finials were often of wood. In fact, many American tall-cased clocks had no finials, the rounded hood or 'bonnet' being decorated with a delicate fret. This has often been damaged or replaced on tall-

FAR LEFT
The brass dial longcase to the left is by an unknown Nottingham clockmaker.

LEFT
Provincial eight-day longcase clock from York. c.1780, with swan-neck pediment and silvered dial.

ABOVE
Thirty-hour brass-dial longcase clock by Adam Brandt of the USA, c.1765.

ABOVE RIGHT
White-dial longcase, c.1810, by Issac Brakaw of Bridge Town, New Jersey. Compare the dial painting here with that of British white dial clocks.

cased clocks found today.

Longcase clocks also achieved a varying degree of popularity throughout continental Europe. In Holland the longcase or 'staande klok' was being made from around 1680 until the early years of the nineteenth century. Dutch longcases often have a 'bombe' shaped base, swelling out towards the base. France had the Normande, a provincial longcase made in Normandy, and longcase versions of the Comtoise, made in the Franche-Comté region, often with a fiddle-shaped case. In Austria the so-called 'Vienna regulator' was occasionally built in a floor standing case. Even Italian and German clock-makers occasionally made longcase clocks.

The most improbable location for a colony of longcase clockmakers must surely be the island of Bornholm off the Danish coast. Here clocks were built which were very similar in style to English longcases. The story goes that the inspiration for these clocks came when a ship bound for Russia with a cargo of British longcases on board came to grief off Bornholm and some of the clocks were washed ashore.

CHAPTER 4

The Search for Precision

SINCE THE earliest days of mechanical horology, innovative clockmakers had been searching for and developing ever more accurate means of measuring time. The great water clock of Su Sung was more accurate than the stick in the sand of the Ancient Egyptians. The anchor escapement was more accurate than the verge. In more recent years, radio-controlled quartz clocks have achieved an accuracy which was literally undreamt of only a few decades ago.

In a way this is only to be expected, given man's natural curiosity and drive to improve on the environment around him. However in the case of horology, there were a number of overriding reasons for developing ever more precise timekeepers: accurate time measurement could be a matter of life or death. As we shall see in a later chapter, it was a fatal accident on the American railways which led to the development of the 'Railroad watch', for example.

Of more immediate significance here were the number of lives lost at sea prior to the development of timekeepers which would perform reliably and accurately for weeks and months aboard a pitching ship in a wide variety of weather conditions. Before the development of such instruments – now known as marine chronometers – shipboard navigation was a chancey business, which depended on the navigator estimating the speed at which his vessel was traveling and the time for which it had traveled. Errors could have disastrous consequences and many sailors lost their lives in shipwrecks. This crude navigational technique was aptly named: it was known as 'dead' reckoning.

The problem was the measurement of longitude. While it was relatively easy to measure latitude at sea – or anywhere else for that matter – by reference to the distance the sun or stars rose above the horizon on a given date, measuring longitude was a much more difficult business. For a given latitude, the night (or day) sky is the same at any longitude – but at different times. In order to measure longitude accurately it is thus necessary to know exactly what time it is.

In the seventeenth and eighteenth centuries, Britain was one of the world's great trading nations – a nation of shopkeepers, as Napoleon put it. International trade required that goods be transported by sea, and a great merchant fleet had developed to service this trade. The losses due to the crudeness of dead reckoning, both in terms of cargo and human life, were immense, and as a result a group of ships' captains petitioned Parliament in 1714 to do something to improve navigation. Parliament's reaction was to pass an Act, signed by Queen Anne, which set up the Board of Longitude and authorized it to offer rewards of up to £20,000 – a huge sum in the early eighteenth century – to anyone who could devise a way of finding a ship's longitude at sea to a specified degree of accuracy.

This challenge was taken up and pursued enthusiastically by John Harrison and, to a lesser extent, his brother James of Barrow-on-Humber. As far as we know, John and James had no formal instruction in clockmaking, having trained in their father's workshop as joiners. This may well have worked to their advantage: they were not locked into conventional horological theory and practice and could perhaps allow their imaginations to range more freely than a trained clockmaker, however brilliant. Their clocks were certainly very different from anything the world had ever seen before and, as we shall see, John Harrison was able to solve problems which even the most skilled clockmaker had no solution to.

One obvious difference in the early Harrison clocks was that they were made almost entirely of wood, reflecting perhaps the training the brothers had received in carpentry. To the modern reader this may seem like a step back: wood cannot be machined as accurately as brass and iron and thus clocks with wooden movements are invariably bulkier than those made of metal. However wood has properties which give it advantages over most metals, one of which is that it does not expand or contract significantly with variations in temperature – expansion and contraction can cause substantial variations in the accuracy of metal movements.

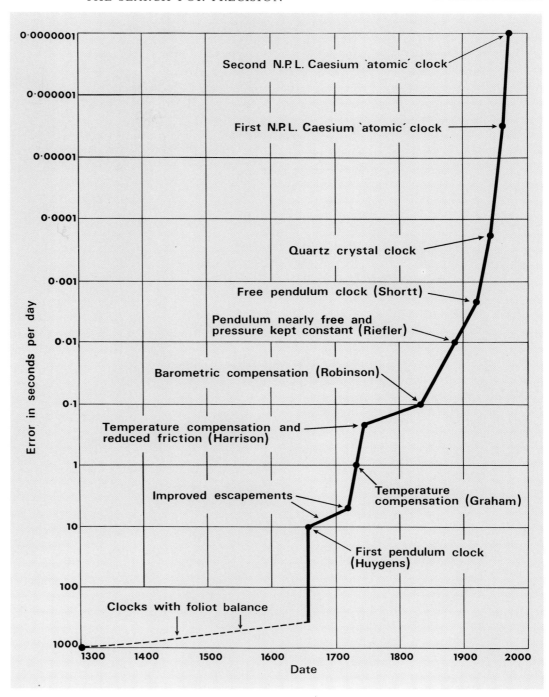

By 1728 the Harrison brothers had completed and tested a prototype 'sea clock' which John Harrison then took to London in the hope of raising money to continue his researches. There he was granted an interview with Edmund Halley, the Astronomer Royal who gave his name to the famous comet. Halley directed Harrison to George Graham, one of London's most illustrious clock-makers, who received him enthusiastically and is said to have lent him £200.

The Harrisons' first clock, made partly of wood and partly of metal was ready for sea trials in 1736 and was installed on a boat to Lisbon. John Harrison himself accompanied the clock on the voyage, at the end of which he was able to give a substantially more accurate estimate of the ship's position than was its captain, who was using

conventional techniques. This success did not entitle John Harrison – now working alone in London, his brother James having returned to Barrow – to any part of the reward offered, as the Act had specified that the measurement of longitude must be done on a voyage to the West Indies. However it encouraged him to continue his researches and persuaded the Commissioners of the Board of Longitude to advance him £500 to build an improved machine.

By 1739, sea clock No 2, an improved version of No 1, had been built and two years later Harrison received another £500 from the Board to produce sea clock No 3, this time to a substantially different design. The complexities of the design of this particular clock must have

caused Harrison, now helped by his son William, many problems, because it was not ready for sea trials until 1759, 17 years after work on it started.

It was Harrison's fourth sea clock – now known as H4 – which finally achieved for him the recognition he so richly deserved, albeit after a long and bitter struggle with the Board of Longitude. H4 was markedly different from any of his previous sea clocks. It looked more like an enormous silver pocket watch than a clock, with a white enamel dial finished with black lettering. The movement of this clock – now, like the others, in the Old Royal Observatory, Greenwich, London – is engraved 'John Harrison & Son', in recognition of the help Harrison had achieved from William.

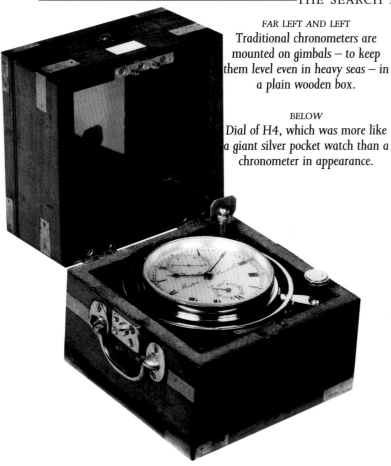

By now Harrison was an old man. He had been born in 1693 and by the time William commenced the voyage to Jamaica in 1761 to give H4 its official trials, he was 68 years of age, having dedicated most of his working life to the problem of finding longitude at sea. On William's arrival in Jamaica eleven-and-a-half weeks later, the watch was found to be only five seconds slow, and under the terms of the Queen Anne Act Harrison became eligible for the £20,000 reward.

The Board of Longitude, influenced perhaps by Harrison's rivals, dug its heels in, seemingly reluctant to part with such a large sum of money without further proof of H4's capabilities. The mechanism of the sea clock was a closely guarded secret of which they knew nothing and they suspected that its performance on the voyage to Jamaica might be nothing more than a fluke. Relations between the Board and Harrison became strained, though they made Harrison an interim award of £2500 and demanded a further trial. This took place in 1764 during a voyage to Barbados and again H4 showed the time correct to under one minute over a period of three months – well within the tolerances specified in the Act. Still the Board was reluctant to pay up, offering to pay half, but only when Harrison revealed the secrets of his design, the other half once Harrison had constructed another timekeeper which performed equally well.

Initially Harrison refused, determined to reveal none of the secrets of his sea clocks until the money had been paid in full. However after a period of months he relented and complied with the first part of the Board's offer. He was paid £7500 – which together with the £2500 he had already received amounted to half the award. Five years later, after H4 had been put through another extensive series of trials by the Board, Harrison had still not received the £10,000 outstanding. By now, however, he and William had completed H5, his fifth and final sea clock. This was tested in the private laboratory of King George III, himself a keen amateur horologist, and found, after ten weeks, to be out by only four and a half seconds. Still the Board hesitated, and it was not until Harrison, with the support of George III, had successfully petitioned Parliament in 1772 – by which time he was almost 80 years old – that the remaining £10,000 was finally paid. Harrison died in March 1776, having made a truly immense contribution to the science of horology.

Harrison's sea clocks were unfortunately too complex and expensive for general shipboard use and as a result other clockmakers began to develop simpler and cheaper timekeepers which did not sacrifice the accuracy of H4. The most important single development in the evolution of these cheaper chronometers was the detent escapement, invented – apparently independently – by Pierre Le Roy in France and by John Arnold and Thomas Earnshaw, both in England.

Arnold and Earnshaw were the first to produce chronometers cheap enough to be used aboard ships in general. Whereas Harrison's sea clocks had taken years to manufacture, Arnold's and Earnshaw's could be made in a matter of weeks. While Arnold's used the pivoted detent escapement and were manufactured in their thousands by Arnold's own company, Earnshaw's incorporated the spring detent which subsequently came into general use as the favored chronometer escapement.

Earnshaw also developed a type of 'compensation' balance. As pointed out earlier, metal has the disadvantage, in terms of clockmaking, that it expands and contracts with variations in temperature. As it expands the escapement will run slow; as it contracts the escapement will run fast. Earnshaw developed a 'bimetallic' balance made of brass and steel which used the differential expansion of these two methods to even out inaccuracies caused by variations in temperature.

Even today, with immensely accurate quartz movements cheaply and abundantly available, marine chronometers are still being made – though they are often bought more by people looking for an unusual clock than by seafarers. Like the traditional chronometers on which they are based, the cylindrical movements of these timekeepers are mounted horizontally on gimbals – a

series of pivots which ensures that the movement stays level even in a boat pitched about by high seas – and cased in a wooden box. It should also be pointed out that in more recent years the word 'chronometer' is also used to denote a wristwatch which has passed a rigorous series of tests laid down by the Swiss authorities.

The other avenue for development of precision timekeepers over the centuries has involved the development of highly accurate pendulum clocks known as 'regulators'. In Britain, most of these take the form of floor-standing 'workshop regulators' in long cases, with a main dial on which are displayed only the minutes, the hours and seconds being indicated on smaller subsidiary dials. In Europe regulators took a variety of forms, the most typical being the 'table regulator' and the wall-mounted 'Vienna regulator' which will be described later. In the United States, the term 'regulator' was often used to describe clocks which did not have a high degree of accuracy, though some American clockmakers did make true regulators.

The problem with conventional clocks was that their design allowed a variety of errors to creep into their time-

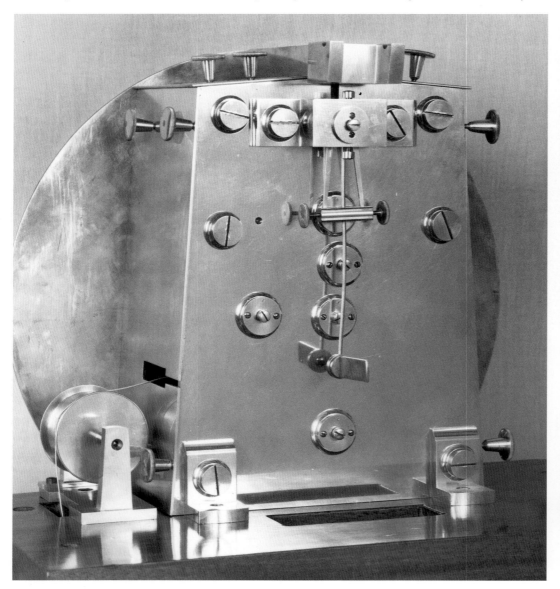

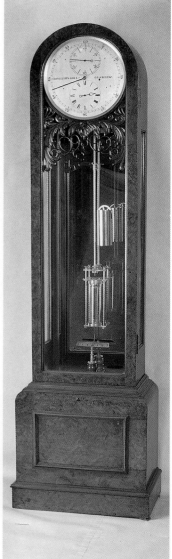

keeping. One of the most obvious of these is that a conventional weight-driven clock stops while it is being wound up (except 30-hour longcase clocks). Clockmakers devised 'maintaining power' systems in which a small spring provides power to keep the clock going while it is being wound.

Another source of error in pendulum clocks came from the fact that a conventional pendulum swings in a circular arc or curve, whereas in order to keep good time it should swing in what is known as a 'cycloidal' arc. Huygens himself, the man who first applied the pendulum to timekeepers, recognized this and devised an arrangement of metal 'cheeks' at the top of the pendulum which forced it to follow a cycloidal curve. Huygens' cheeks were not widely used by clockmakers, who soon realized that for small arcs of travel the cycloidal and circular arcs were very similar and much work then went into ensuring that regulator pendulums had a very short swing.

As we have seen with chronometers, the expansion and contraction of metals with variations in temperature are a potential source of error. The same is true with regulators. Here the error comes about when a rise in temperature causes the pendulum rod to expand and the clock to run slow – and vice versa. Clockmakers have devised a great many ways of compensating for this error. One of the simplest was to make the pendulum rod of wood, and it is something of a mystery why this method was not adopted by more makers of longcase clocks in Britain. Wooden rods were used extensively by Austrian clockmakers – most Vienna regulators have wooden pendulum rods. In more recent years alloys such as Invar have been developed which have a low 'coefficient of expansion' – their size does not change much with variations in temperature.

One of the first methods of temperature compensation for pendulum clocks was devised by John Harrison. Harrison's compensation involved using the differential effect of brass rods expanding in an upwards direction to compensate for steel ones expanding downwards. A 'gridiron' pendulum using this form of compensation is very distinctive, the 'rod' actually consisting of an array of rods – usually nine – alternately of steel and brass.

Another popular pendulum compensation system was devised by the London clockmaker George Graham, who, as we have seen earlier, was one of the first to recognize Harrison's abilities. In place of the conventional lead-filled brass bobs, Graham used a glass cylinder containing mercury. The upward expansion of the mercury in the cylinder effectively compensated for the downward expansion of the steel pendulum rod. Both the gridiron and the mercury pendulums had the added advantage of being visually attractive in their own right and were for this reason often used even in clocks which were not strictly precision timekeepers.

The anchor escapement was another source of error in many pendulum clocks; its geometry causes the clock train to be pushed backwards slightly with each swing of

FAR LEFT
Movement of traditional workshop regulator by Lecomber. Note the high quality finish of all components.

ABOVE
William IV mahogany and ebony regulator. Note the mercury compensated pendulum.

LEFT
The Lecomber regulator was made for a Glasgow clockmaker. It is in an unusual walnut veneered case.

the pendulum. You can see this happening by watching the seconds hand of a conventional longcase. With each 'tick' of the clock the seconds hand moves forward one division and then very slightly backwards. To counteract this escapement error, Graham devised the 'dead-beat' escapement, which causes the train to stop dead with each tick but does not push it backwards. The dead-beat escapement, which has a very small arc of swing, is often used in regulators.

The gravity escapement was devised to counteract the effects of another major source of error in mechanical clocks – the variation in power supplied to the escapement via the wheels in the going train. If the power increased, the pendulum would receive a greater impulse, would swing further and take longer, and the clock would run slow. If the power decreased, the clock would run fast. The gravity escapement got round this by providing impulse to the escapement *indirectly* via a 'gravity arm'. The arm is lifted by the impulsing power of the escape wheel. It then falls under the influence of gravity – which is constant – and in so doing impulses the pendulum. The gravity arm can be seen as serving a similar purpose to the 'remontoire' in spring-driven clocks. A remontoire is a mechanism containing a small spring which is rewound at short intervals – every minute, for example – by the going train. The escape wheel is then driven by power from the remontoire and thus is not exposed to the variations in power as the mainspring winds down. The fusee, which will be described in Chapter 5, serves a similar purpose in spring-driven clocks.

ABOVE LEFT
Vienna-type wall regulators like this used a variety of devices to improve timekeeping, one of which – visible here – was an elliptical wooden pendulum rod.

LEFT
Atmos clocks like this one use changes in barometric pressure and temperature to wind the mainspring. They are thus capable of running for a virtually indefinite period without any attention whatsoever.

RIGHT
A 90-day workshop regulator made by E Howard & Co of Boston, Massachussetts.

FAR RIGHT
Longcase regulator by Ferdinand Berthoud of Paris, 1802.

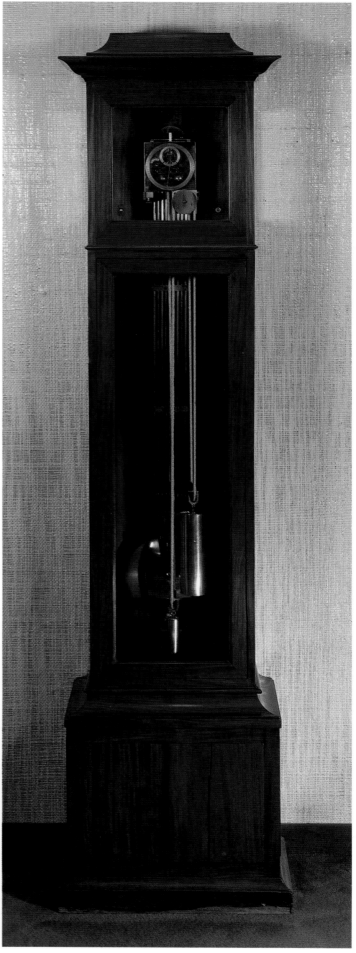

LEFT
Astronomical clock by Samuel Watson of Coventry and London, Mathematician in Ordinary to King Charles II.

RIGHT
Reconstruction of Giovanni de Dondi's famous astronomical clock.

BELOW
Back plate of the Watson astronomical clock.

One of the most effective ways of dealing with variations in the power delivered by the going train to the escape wheel is to ensure that these do not occur in the first place. This can be done, for example, by manufacturing the parts from which the train is made very precisely, by ensuring that the moving parts are as light as possible, and by providing pivot holes with 'bushes' which do not wear quickly. One common way of doing the last of these is by 'jeweling' the going train, something which is commonly done with regulators and chronometers – as well as high quality watch movements. The jewels used, usually industrial rubies nowadays, are tiny rings like donuts mounted in the plates. The pivot runs directly in the donut hole.

The typical regulator would incorporate a combination of these features. The parts, particularly the wheels, would all be made to a fine level of tolerance. The escapement would be dead-beat and the pendulum would have some form of compensation. The wheels – or at least some of them – would run in jeweled pivot holes.

All of these methods have been used throughout the years to enhance the performance of timekeepers, and in combination they were used in the construction of regulators whose performance was not equalled until the advent of quartz technology in the second half of the twentieth century.

CHAPTER 5

Bracket, Mantel and Shelf

BRACKET, MANTEL and shelf clocks, in their diverse and fully evolved forms, are very different in style, period and place of manufacture. Spring-driven bracket clocks, for example, were made mainly in England, France and Japan. In England bracket clocks in wooden cases were introduced around the same time as the pendulum, 1670, and were made, in changing styles, until Edwardian times. In France recognizable bracket clocks appeared a few years later, in a very different form, often in ornate cases with a form of marquetry and metal inlay known as Boulle work. Japanese bracket clocks are very different again, these normally being in brass cases and having twin escapements and adjustable hour markers to cope with the Japanese system of 'unequal hours' (daylight hours being of a different length from night hours).

The term 'mantel clock' covers a wide range of clocks, for the most part smaller in size than bracket clocks. These include carriage clocks, French black marble clocks, 400-day clocks, skeleton clocks, the ubiquitous 'Napoleon's Hat' clock and many many more, both mechanically and electrically driven. The sheer variety of mantel clock types makes comprehensive coverage impossible in a book of this kind, and only the most popular styles will be described.

Weight-driven shelf clocks were an American development, their construction reflecting the scarcity of certain raw materials in nineteenth century America. Again, these were produced in a large variety of styles, only the most important of which will be dealt with here.

The bracket clock, with its plated movement was essentially a development of the Continental table clock in an upright case, which appeared as a direct result of the application of the pendulum to clocks. The typical early English bracket clock is a rather grand affair and would have been owned by someone with plenty of money who could afford what in those days must have been something of an executive toy. Early bracket clocks are thought to have been made with a matching wall bracket on which they stood, though original brackets are very rare today. The term 'bracket clock' is in fact of more

ABOVE
Clockmaking during the French decorative arts movement drew on the services of a great variety of craftsmen, including sculptors, gilders, metalworkers and cabinetmakers.

RIGHT
English eight-day bracket clock c.1790, with fusee and verge escapement. Note the elaborately engraved back plate of the movement.

LEFT
Eight-day shelf clock by E N Welch Manufacturing Co, Connecticut, c.1885.

recent origin: at the time of manufacture these clocks were known as 'spring clocks' to distinguish them from the other clock types in the clockmaker's repertoire: weight-driven, longcase and lantern.

The spring-driven movement of the bracket clock uses a 'fusee' to compensate for the gradual loss of power as the spring, contained in a brass 'barrel', runs down. Coiled springs develop their maximum power when they are fully wound, when all of the coils are wrapped tightly round the central arbor. As the spring unwinds, the power output gradually lessens, the impulse delivered to the pendulum falls and the arc of swing of the pendulum becomes smaller. Result: the clock begins to run faster.

The fusee is a cone-shaped piece of brass which carries the main wheel of the going train and is attached to the spring barrel by a line of gut or a chain similar to a miniature bicycle chain. When the clock is run down, the chain is wrapped around the spring barrel. When the fusee is turned, it gathers up the chain, winding the spring as it does so. The coiled spring then exerts force on the gut or chain which, as the clock runs, gradually winds off the fusee and back on to the barrel. As the spring runs down and its power diminishes, the gut or chain bears on a wider and wider part of the fusee cone and, by the laws of leverage, needs less power to turn the fusee. Thus it compensates for the loss of power from the spring.

Bracket clock movements were substantially built, usually with strike, often with chime, and occasionally with music work and the ability to play any one of a selection of tunes on the hour. In the early days the back plates of bracket clocks were elaborately engraved, usually with an overall pattern of foliage and scrolls around the maker's name and the place of manufacture. Later makers dispensed with such elaborate engraving as it was rarely seen.

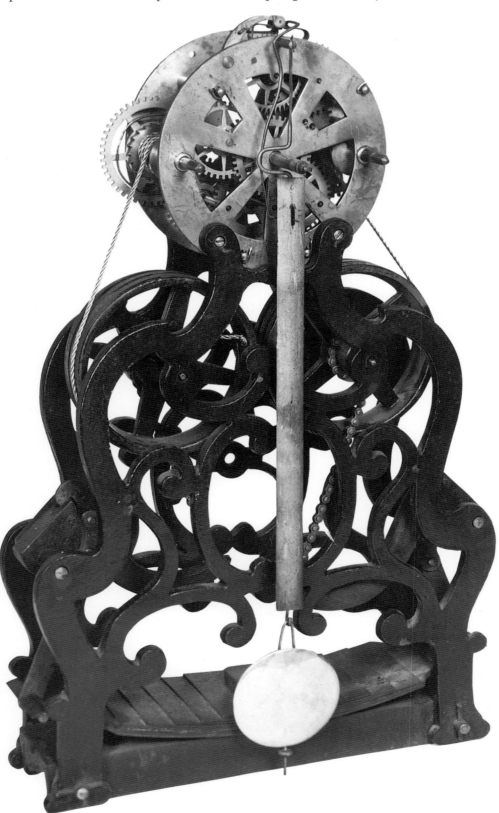

LEFT
Movement of a wagon-spring clock. The power to drive this clock comes from the leaf spring mounted in the base and is transmitted via a chain-and-lever arrangement to the movement.

RIGHT
Regency style bracket clock in mahogany and brass made by Ebenezer Handscomb of Woburn.

FAR RIGHT
George III mahogany bracket clock by Robert Henderson of London. The subsidiary dial in the arch can be used for silencing the strike.

The cases of early bracket clocks – like those of early longcase clocks – mimicked the styles of classical architecture, with triangular pediments, columns on either side of the dial topped off with Corinthian capitals in brass, and other applied brass decorations. Most of these clocks had brass dials with silvered brass chapter rings and cast brass corner decorations or spandrels. The dial center, inside the chapter ring, was normally matted. Often the dials of bracket clocks would include a small aperture which allowed a small 'mock pendulum' to be seen, swinging gaily to and fro. This was carried on an extension of the pallet arbor of the verge escapement.

Incidentally, even until well after the introduction of the anchor escapement, these clocks continued to be manufactured with the less accurate verge. The reason for this may be that the bracket was seen at the time as a 'portable' clock. Most early brackets had a carrying handle on top of the case and could be carried from room to room. The verge escapement, less liable to damage and less fussy about being placed on a level surface, was more portable than the anchor.

As the years progressed, the styles of bracket clocks followed the changing fashions of the times. Cases at first became more elaborate and ornamental, perhaps under the influence of the French decorative arts movement, and then – beginning in the Regency period (1810-1820) – developed along much simpler lines without the fussy carved decorations of the earlier period.

Around the middle of the eighteenth century a new type of dial was developed, the silvered dial. Unlike the earlier brass dials with its separate chapter rings and separate applied spandrels, this new dial was made from a single piece of brass silvered all over and with the hour markings simply engraved into its front surface, the engraving being filled with black wax to make it stand out. Later still, bracket clocks appeared with enamelled dials, normally circular and white with black markings.

By this time the bracket clock had become smaller, mantelpieces had become a feature of houses throughout Europe, and a great variety of small spring-driven clocks began to appear on these mantelpieces, particularly in France. One of the most popular of these new mantel clocks was the carriage clock, first made in the early years of the nineteenth century by the great and innovative French clockmaker Abraham-Louis Breguet.

The typical carriage clock has a small spring-driven movement controlled by a lever or a cylinder escapement mounted on a platform across the plates on top of the

George I ebony bracket clock with
inverted bell top. This clock has
grande sonnerie striking – it
strikes both hours and quarters at
each quarter.

RIGHT
Boulle-cased bracket clock by
Thomas Tompion. Boulle was
invented by the Frenchman Andre
Charles Boulle and consists of a
base material, usually
tortoiseshell, with inlay work,
usually brass.

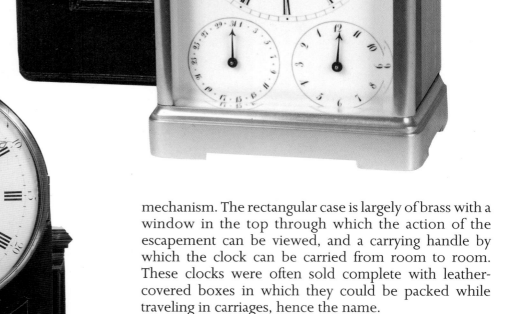

mechanism. The rectangular case is largely of brass with a window in the top through which the action of the escapement can be viewed, and a carrying handle by which the clock can be carried from room to room. These clocks were often sold complete with leather-covered boxes in which they could be packed while traveling in carriages, hence the name.

While it was Breguet who invented these *pendules de voyage*, it was up to another Frenchman, a Parisian clock-maker called Paul Garnier, to put this clock style into mass production and in so doing to establish the Parisian carriage clock industry. Following the phenomenal popularity of these clocks, many other French clock-makers began to make carriage clocks, the popularity of which went far beyond France, and led to the construction of clocks of this type in other countries.

In Britain, for example, clockmakers such as James McCable, Thomas Cole and Justin Vulliamy were build-ing carriage clocks, normally larger and heavier than their French counterparts, for the luxury market. The Swiss,

like the British, were quick to jump on the carriage clock bandwagon, early Swiss models having been found which date from the second decade of the nineteenth century. By the third decade, clocks which were recognizably in the carriage clock style were being made in Austria, and by the end of the century, mass-produced carriage clocks aimed at the cheaper end of the market were being produced in both Germany and America, then the largest clock production centers in the world.

The clockmakers of America and Germany also made their own copies of another phenomenally popular type of French mantel clock, a type which has now become known, because of the materials used in the construction of the case, as the 'French black marble', though the cases of the vast majority of these clocks are in fact made from Belgian slate, polished to a high gloss finish.

These clocks were manufactured in France towards the end of the nineteenth century and were an immediate success, particularly in Britain where the color black had become more prevalent when prolonged periods of mourning became more common, following Queen Victoria's example after the death of the Prince Consort in 1861. These clocks were often made in architectural form, with a triangular pediment supported by columns on either side. The dials were circular, often with a porcelain chapter ring. Cheaper copies of these clocks were made by clockmaking companies like Junghans in Germany, where they were often cased on wood painted black and polished to resemble marble, and Ansonia in the United States, cased in cast iron or, occasionally, black slate inlaid with marble.

Mechanically speaking, French black marble clocks are excellent timekeepers, the drum-shaped movements normally being finished to a very high standard. Many are still available today at reasonable prices and, in most cases, the movements are still capable of being salvaged and the clocks still capable of giving many years good service. The cases are often in poor condition, though these too can usually be redeemed by skilled restoration. German and American examples are generally of poorer quality though these too are often still capable of giving good service for many years to come.

The American clockmaking industry also produced mantel clocks – or 'shelf clocks' as they were known – of types which were wholly American in style. Shelf clocks took over from wooden movement longcases as the clock which less wealthy Americans could afford. The style was first invented around 1812 by Eli Terry of Plymouth, Connecticut, the man who is credited with first bringing the techniques of mass production to the clockmaking industry.

Terry's early shelf clocks were housed in plain rectangular wooden cases with a glass door in front which allowed the movement and pendulum to be seen. The first models had no dial, the hour markings being simply painted on the reverse of the glass door, thus continuing a tradition of painted glass in American horology dating back to Simon Willard's 'banjo'.

These early shelf clocks still had wooden movements, now with the escape wheel and pendulum in front, allowing the action of the escapement to be seen through the glass door. Unlike European mantel clocks, American shelf clocks were weight driven, the weights being suspended on lines which ran over pulleys in the top of the case. This allowed the weights sufficient fall to run the clocks for a whole day. Later models of Terry's shelf clocks had a true dial and less austere 'pillar and scroll' cases, with pillars either side and scrolled moldings top and bottom.

It was Chauncey Jerome, who had at one time worked in Terry's factory, who introduced the brass movement to the shelf clock genre and in so doing opened a new chapter in American clockmaking tradition. Jerome invented the clock which probably became the most important American clock type, a clock which was to sweep all before it as the nineteenth century moved into its second half. This is the clock now known as the 'OG' or 'ogee', a name it takes from the ogive molding which runs round the front edge of the rectangular case. Like Terry, Jerome used a glass door at the front of the case, though the movement was now hidden behind a dial – as in the later Terry shelf clocks – and the pendulum behind a painted glass tablet in the lower half of the door.

In any consideration of American horology in the nineteenth century it must be pointed out that an overriding factor was a shortage of certain raw materials, particularly mainsprings and brass. Spring steel was virtually impossible to obtain, so the vast majority of clocks were weight-driven, and brass was in very short supply. As a result of the latter, Jerome's movements were very frugal in their use of brass, setting a trend which was to be followed by American clockmakers in years to come. His movement plates were thin, with excess brass being cut out where it was not needed. The wheels, too, were thin, having grooves stamped around their perimeter for extra strength.

The ogee was probably the most popular American mechanical clock ever made. Clocks of this type were made in their thousands by Jerome and a variety of other American clockmakers: Seth Thomas, Brewster & Ingrahams, the Waterbury Clock Company and others. They were exported in vast quantities to Europe, in the process destroying the traditional Black Forest clock-making industry. They can still be picked up for a reasonable price at auctions and fit in well with modern interiors. Though originally made to stand on a shelf, ogees are now normally hung on the wall.

No discussion of mantel clocks would be complete without reference to the 'Napoleon's Hat,' a clock style which became popular in the early twentieth century. Napoleon's Hat clocks – so called because the cases of these clocks resembled the three-cornered hats worn by Napoleon and others – were made in Britain and Germany, and possibly in America. They had sturdily made spring-driven pendulum movements, normally with striking on a gong laid along the base of the clock, often with chime. Dismissed until recently, like many other mechanical clock types of the nineteenth and twentieth centuries, as cheap mass-produced ephemera, Napoleon's Hat clocks are now coming back into fashion as collectables from the interwar period.

ABOVE LEFT
An American copy of the ubiquitous French black marble clock – the cases of which were actually made from highly polished black Belgian slate. The case of this particular clock, made by Ansonia, c.1902, is actually made of wood painted to simulate slate.

RIGHT
This 'triple-decker' shelf clock was made by C & N Jerome of Bristol, Connecticut, c.1835.

LEFT
A 'steeple on steeple' or 'double steepled' shelf clock with a 30-hour brass movement. The name is a reference to the shape of the case.

CHAPTER 6

France and the Decorative Arts

AS EVEN the most casual observer of today's auctionroom merry-go-round can hardly fail to have noticed, France is the home of the decorative arts, a movement which began in the time of Louis XIV, *le Roi Soleil*, and went on right through the eighteenth and nineteenth centuries. It brought about the baroque revival in the eighteenth century, gave rise to the rococo styles of Louis XIV and Louis XV and even manifested itself in the late nineteenth century Art Nouveau style and Art Deco style of the 1920s and 1930s. Generally, it is typefied by lavish and elaborate decoration, drawing often on nature and classical and mythological themes for its inspiration.

The decorative arts movement made use of the talents of a great variety of craftsmen and extended to all types of furnishing items, clocks included. One major effect on horology was that the case became more important than the clock, the casemaker more important than the clock-maker, the clock more important as a piece of decorative furniture than as a useful precision instrument, a machine for measuring the passage of time. Clock cases were elaborately and highly decorated, and were regarded as much as works of art in many cases as the paintings and sculptures which decorated the French homes and gardens of the time. Cases were made of an enormous variety of materials, including gilt, ormolu, enamel, metal, Boulle, porcelain – and even wood. Their manufacture might involve calling on the services of the artist, the sculptor, the potter, the gilder, the metalworker, the cabinetmaker – each an artist in his own field. Clocks as items of furniture surely reached their apogee in seventeenth to nineteenth century France.

In fact, clockmaking in France began centuries prior to this. While the origins of the mechanical clock are now obscure, it seems certain that France played a major role in the early development of horology and it is likely that the clockmakers who built the early English turret clocks – such as those at Salisbury and Wells – were French in origin. Many of the horological terms which have come down to us have their roots in the French language. The very word 'horology', for example, is derived from the

ABOVE
Highly decorative French mantel clock in an oak case veneered with ebony and tortoiseshell with gilt-bronze mounts.

RIGHT
Elaborately decorated French mantel clock by Ferdinand Berthoud of Paris.

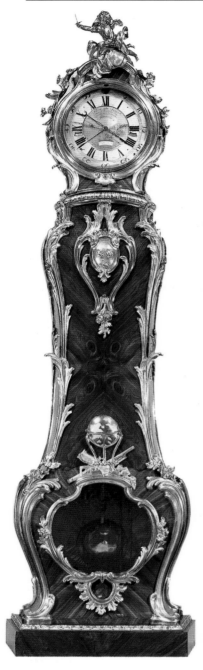

ABOVE
This French longcase regulator by
Samson Le Roy of Paris, c.1755,
could hardly be more different
from the austere workshop
regulators of the British. The
kingwood veneered case of this
clock was made by Balthazar
Lieutaud.

French *horloge*, a clock. Another example is the word 'arbor', used to describe the spindle which runs through clock wheels and pinions. This comes from the French *arbre*, a tree; the original arbors were probably made of wood.

When the coiled mainspring was introduced as a power source for domestic timekeepers in the fifteenth century, French clockmakers adopted it wholeheartedly. Thus the typical French clock, if such a thing exists, is surely the spring-driven table or mantel clock, just as the 'typical' British clock is the weight-driven longcase, the 'typical' German clock the weight-driven wall clock and the 'typical' American clock the weight-driven shelf clock.

By the end of the sixteenth century, when domestic clockmaking was just beginning, the French clock-making industry was already highly developed, produc-ing fine spring-driven table clocks. In the seventeenth century, French clockmaking came under the influence of the more sober and puritanical Dutch, at that time a country very much at the forefront of scientific progress. Christiaan Huygens, a pivotal figure in world horology, actually lived in Paris for some years. Dutch clock styles were adapted for French needs, particularly a clock

which the Dutch had recently introduced called a *Haags klokje* or Hague clock, a small spring-driven clock in a very plain wooden case with little in the way of decoration. While early Hague clocks were wall-mounted, later examples were made as table or bracket clocks.

The French version of the Hague clock became known as the *pendule religieuse* because of its austere appearance. As the decorative arts movement took hold, however, the appearance of French mantel clocks became more and more ornate, more and more elaborately decorated – and around this time French clockmaking began to diverge into two separate but parallel branches. One in-volved the production of elaborately cased clocks, works of art in themselves, in which the movement was of rela-tively little importance: the case was the clock. The other involved clockmakers who chose to push out the boun-daries of horological progress, producing highly com-plex and accurate clocks, clocks which incorporated many ingenious and important mechanical innovations.

The movements of decorative clocks were relatively simple in construction, though they were generally built to a very good standard and had a high quality of finish. They were bought by the casemakers from movement makers in Paris, then the center of the French clock-

LEFT
A Hague clock – or 'Haags klokje' – by Salomon Coster of the Hague. Clocks like these were used as the basis of the French pendule religieuse.

ABOVE LEFT
Louis XVI ormolu and terracotta mantel clock signed 'Sotiau à Paris'.

RIGHT
Charles X ormolu and malachite mantel clock. The sculpture shows the brothers Horatii taking their oath after David.

making industry, before being mounted in the cases and sold. As the years progressed, these movements – *pendules de Paris*, as they became known – settled down into a consistent form, with circular highly polished plates, very fine pivots, anchor escapements, rack-and-snail striking; they were powered by a long spring in a 'going' barrel without a fusee. The extra-long mainspring is a way of compensating for the lack of a power equalisation device such as a fusee. Though it gives these French clocks a going period of approximately a fortnight, they are classified as eight-day clocks on the basis that the power output from the mainspring is relatively consistent during the first week. In the second, timekeeping becomes very erratic. The advantage of these movements is that they are fairly accurate and at the same time relatively cheap to produce, hence their popularity.

By the nineteenth century these movements were being produced in huge quantities to satisfy the demands of both the home market and the exporters, though for the most part they were now no longer made in Paris, being built instead in the new clock factories of Montbéliard and St Nicholas d'Aliermont. In 1818 Frederic Japy had established a factory for movements at Badeval in Montbéliard near the Swiss-French border and here produced thousand upon thousand of *pendule de Paris* movements, many of which are still keeping good time today. A substantial number of these movements crossed the English Channel to be mounted in British cases and sold, often with the name of the retailer of the dial. Other makers followed Japy's example: Jean Vincenti who set up his factory in 1823, for example, and Samuel Marti. By this time many of these movements were being incorporated in the black marble clocks described earlier.

The construction of complex mechanical clocks in France was pioneered by clockmakers such as Julien Le Roy who, in 1736 built a complex clock which showed the 'equation of time', the difference between clock time (or 'mean' time) and sun time, which can differ by as much as 15 minutes per day depending on the time of year. Le Roy's son Pierre did pioneering work on marine chronometers involving the development of compensated balances and a type of detent escapement. This innovative work was carried on by Ferdinand Berthoud, one of the elder Le Roy's apprentices, and by the greatest French clockmaker of all, Abraham-Louis Breguet.

Breguet was born in Neuchâtel, Switzerland, in 1747, though his parents are thought to have been of French Protestant origin. At the age of 18, the young Abraham traveled to Paris where he was apprenticed as a watchmaker under several masters, possibly including Lepine and Berthoud – both clockmakers to the King - and then under Etienne Gide. During this period, Brequet was attending lectures on mathematics at the College Mazarin studies which must have stood him in great stead in his later career. In 1775, now 28, Breguet married Marie-Louise l'Huillier, daughter of a respected Parisian family, and soon afterwards used her dowry to set up his own

LEFT
French Empire clocks such as this, made c.1810, were often influenced by classical themes.

BELOW LEFT
Nineteenth century French elephant mantel clock by the Parisian clockmaker Thuret.

RIGHT
Empire ormolu mantel clock. The sculpture is representative of the Arts and Sciences.

BELOW
Swiss lever watch with tourbillon escapement invented by Breguet. In this type of movement the escapement is mounted in a revolving carriage to help eliminate positional errors.

workshop at Versailles in partnership with Gide's brother Xavier, a relationship which lasted until 1791. In fact, by 1793 the Revolution had driven Breguet and his son Antoine Louis back to Neuchâtel, though by 1795 they were back in Paris, and had re-established the Versailles factory. Soon the workshops were employing 100 people, and producing a variety of high-class and reliable clocks and watches.

Breguet made many innovations in watchmaking and clockmaking. For example, in 1780 he produced the first 'automatic' or self-winding watch. Movements of the wearer's body caused an eccentric weight within the watch to swivel and in so doing to keep the movement wound up. The watch was said to be capable of going for eight years without overhaul. Another Breguet development was the first 'tact' watch, which allowed the wearer to tell the time by touching the hands and dial. Such watches were of considerable importance not only to people with visual disabilities, but also to fully sighted people in the days before reliable electric lighting.

Breguet also invented the tourbillon, a type of escapement fitted inside a cage which revolves as the watch goes. One of the problems with watches was that their timekeeping accuracy tended to vary depending on

65

whether the escapement was in the face-up position, the face-down position or any position in between. The tourbillon, by keeping the escapement itself moving through a variety of positions, effectively compensates for such 'positional errors'.

One of Breguet's best-known innovations was one which had more to do with the way in which watches were sold than with horological technology. This was the *souscription* or 'subscription' watch, so called because it was paid for by subscription. The buyer paid a proportion of the cost of the watch in advance, the remainder being payable when the watch was finished.

In general, Breguet's clocks and watches were more austere and less decorative than those of his contemporaries, perhaps reflecting his Protestant upbringing. His subscription watches, however, were to set new standards of simplicity – and therefore cost. Breguet used fewer parts and batch production methods to keep the costs down. And although two-handed watches were by now the order of the day, Breguet's subscription watches had only a single hour hand.

The clock (and watch) which must surely rate as Breguet's masterpiece was his *pendule sympathique*, the first of which was made in the early years of the nineteenth century. This was a mantel or table clock with a receptacle on top in which a special pocket watch could be mounted. At a given time, the clock would not only wind and set the watch to time, but would automatically regulate it for any error. These clocks, of which a number were made, appear to have been used by Breguet as promotional tools. Breguet died in 1823. The firm continued

LEFT
A Breguet pendule sympathique. The watch is placed in a receptacle above the clock to be rewound, reset and regulated.

ABOVE RIGHT
A fine French empire pendule squelette signed 'Breguet'.

RIGHT
A nineteenth century ormolu and porcelain garniture set of clock and candelabra.

under his son and in fact still exists today, though it has gone through several changes of ownership.

No account of French horology would be complete without mention of provincial clockmaking, the products of which were seldom exported and thus do not often turn up outside France. These include the clock now normally known as the *Comtoise* – also called the *Morez* or *Morbier* – which was first produced in the Franche-Comté region around the middle of the eighteenth century. Early Comtoise clocks had a verge escapement though later models used the anchor. Many Comtoise clocks were wall-hanging, and many more were built with floor-standing long cases. The Comtoise was the most popular of all French provincial clocks, selling throughout France, normally with the name of the retailer, rather than that of the maker, on the dial.

France also gave rise to another, more localized, type of provincial longcase, the *Normande*, which appeared, as the name suggests, in Normandy. These were produced in a great variety of case styles, many of which had a swelling and lenticle half-way down the trunk to allow the pendulum bob to be seen as it swung to and fro. Eventually, the Normande clock movement was replaced by that of the Comtoise, and the clock existed as a case-style alone.

Production of the Comtoise reached its peak in the middle of the nineteenth century. Following its defeat in the Franco-Prussian War, 1870/71, France lifted the tax on German goods and in so doing allowed a great influx into the country of cheap Black Forest clocks. This led to the decline of the provincial French clockmaking industry and by the outbreak of the First World War, production of the Comtoise had all but ceased.

FAR LEFT
A typical 'Comtoise' or 'Morbier' wall clock from the nineteenth century. The pendulum hangs in front of the weights, hiding them. This clock strikes the hours, then repeats the striking two minutes later.

LEFT
A French Empire-style clock, c.1830, with highly embellished brass decoration.

RIGHT
This type of French clock, with glass panels on four sides of the case, is known appropriately enough as a 'four-glass' clock. American versions were called 'crystal regulators'. The visible dead-beat Brocot escapement and mercury compensated pendulum were used more for decorative effect than for precision timekeeping.

CHAPTER 7

Germany and the Black Forest

FROM A very early date after the invention of the first mechanical clock somewhere in Central Europe, German clockmakers were active in developing horological technology. Such was the skill of these clockmakers that public buildings and churches in southern Germany soon housed clocks with highly complex astronomical movements.

The great centers of clockmaking in Germany in the early years were Augsburg and Nuremberg, both of which lie in the southern German province of Bavaria. Augsburg was best known for the manufacture of clocks incorporating moving figures or automata. Nuremberg was better known for the production of small portable clocks and small portable ivory sundials. It was also the home of Peter Henlein, the man often credited with having made the first watches. These were oval in shape and known as 'Nuremberg eggs'. Henlein is also the earliest known clockmaker to have used the fusee. The ivory sundials were made by a variety of craftsmen during the sixteenth and seventeenth centuries and are now highly prized.

It was during the seventeenth century that the craft of clockmaking was introduced into the Black Forest area of Southern Germany. Legend has it that the industry arose as a result of a wooden wheeled clock movement being brought into the area by a traveler from Bohemia. Local peasant farmers, who commonly spent the inhospitable winter months doing woodcarving, made their own versions of this clock and, having satisfied local demand, began to 'export' the clocks out of the Black Forest area. From the beginning, clockmakers in the Black Forest aimed at the cheaper end of the market, producing clocks which were simple, robust and without pretension – though not particularly precise in their timekeeping abilities.

Most of these early Black Forest clocks were weight-driven wall clocks. Very little metal was used in their construction. The movement frame was wooden as were the majority of wheels and arbors, though the pivots at either end of the arbors were of wire The escape wheel

had wire pins instead of teeth and the verge was made of bent wire, the escapement being controlled by a wooden foliot. The clocks were driven by a weight – a stone or a piece of iron – suspended below the movement. The dial, which was often arched in the fashion of British and American longcase clocks, was of wood, painted white with black numerals and a colored pattern of floral

RIGHT
A complex astronomical automaton clock made near Strasbourg in the Black Forest, c.1620.

LEFT
Most early Black Forest clocks had weight-driven movements made almost entirely of wood.

LEFT
An eighteenth century weight-driven wall clock made in Northern Germany.

BELOW
A single-handed hexagonal brass table clock from seventeenth century Augsburg.

RIGHT
The porcelain factories of Meissen, Germany, supplied colorful and highly decorative clock cases.

1925-679

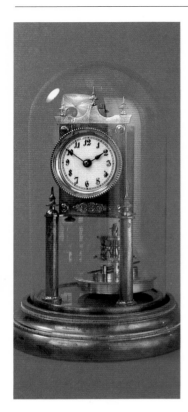

LEFT
Germany was the center of production of 400-day, or anniversary clocks like these.

BELOW
Organ clocks like this were manufactured in the Black Forest from c.1770. This type of clock played a short tune on the hour, as well as, or in place of, striking.

RIGHT
A German iron 'jack' clock. The jack is the figure sitting on top of the movement which strikes the bells.

decoration in the corners and the arch. The dials of Black Forest clocks destined for the British market were often circular with a mahogany surround, in imitation of the then-popular English dial.

In the eighteenth century the foliot gave way to the pendulum, which was generally short and hung in front of the dial, giving rise to the popular name 'cow's tail pendulum'. The clocks acquired strike work, the striking train being positioned behind the going train in the manner of British lantern clocks. As the century progressed, the short pendulum and verge escapement of these clocks was replaced with the long pendulum and anchor escapement, now positioned behind the dial, as well as brass wheels, though the frames and arbors were still made of wood.

In the early years, clockmaking in the Black Forest was organized very much on a 'cottage industry' basis, with outworkers producing the clocks manually in their own homes, the clocks being distributed by traveling salesmen who loaded themselves up with clocks and wandered off into the European hinterland, returning only after they had sold their stock, a process which sometimes took years. As the industry matured, the salesmen settled down in towns outside the area, outside Germany, importing clocks from the Black Forest and selling them in the local community. Soon a complex network of Black Forest agents had developed which penetrated Europe's darkest corners and by the early nineteenth century the Black Forest was the world's premier clockmaking center, particularly for low-priced clocks, which were soon available all over Europe.

In the middle of the nineteenth century disaster struck, in the form of competition from the American clockmaking industry, which a few decades earlier had started to reorganize itself, producing clocks in factories using the techniques of mass-production first introduced by Eli Terry in 1807. The Black Forest industry, still organized on a cottage-industry basis, began to suffer as these cheaper and more reliable machine-made clocks, particularly the ogee, were imported en masse into Europe. As sales collapsed, the Black Forest clockmaking industry began to reorganize itself along American lines, a long and sometimes painful process. Outworkers forsook their independence and moved into factories producing clocks which, at first, were little more than copies of American factory-made clocks, though as the years went by a variety of clock types appeared which were more typically Black Forest in origin.

By the end of the century, the industry had re-established itself and once again was the world's premier clockmaking center. Its success in so doing was based in so small part on a new clock design, the so-called 'postman's alarm', which was exported in great numbers to fulfill the demands of the British market. Like the earlier Black Forest clocks on which it was based, the postman's alarm was a weight-driven wall clock. It had alarm work where the striking train would normally have been and a

LEFT
A German weight-driven wall
clock, c.1900, in the style of a
*Vienna regulator, but
incorporating shelves on either
side of the case.*

FAR RIGHT
This elegant month-going
German wall regulator
incorporates a center sweep
seconds hand and a gridiron
pendulum.

BELOW RIGHT
Talking clocks were invented by
Bernhard Hiller of Berlin. This
example dates from c.1910.

long chain to allow the alarm an extended ringing period. The movement still had wooden frames, though other parts of the clock, including the arbors, were now of metal. The alarm bell sat on top of the movement, more or less hidden by the circular dial. The weights, like those of the now-popular cuckoo clock were in the shape of pine cones. No-one now knows why the name 'postman's alarm' was coined to describe these clocks. Perhaps the postman, who rose earlier in the morning than most, required a longer ring to make sure he woke up.

Another highly popular type of factory-made Black Forest clock was the 'Regulator', based on the Vienna regulator, though the majority of Black Forest regulators, particularly later examples, were spring- rather than weight-driven and lack the precision movements of their Austrian cousins. One common feature of the Black Forest regulators is the gridiron or mock gridiron pendulum rod: the vast majority of Vienna regulators have plain wooden or steel rods. Another distinguishing feature is the pendulum bob which often carries the letters 'R' (for 'Retard') and 'A' (for 'Advance') in Gothic script, indicating that the rate can be altered by screwing the rating nut to the left or the right.

Many German factory regulators are very similar in overall appearance to the Vienna clocks from which they are derived, though as the years passed there was a tendency for the clocks to become plainer in appearance. Ultimately these clocks were cased in little more than

LEFT
A South German crucifix clock. The movement is in the base, while the time is indicated by a stationary pointer on a revolving band around the sphere on the top of the cross.

ABOVE
Black Forest picture clocks. c.1860.

been trained to build in Austria. Becker's clocks enjoyed great success for a number of decades and still turn up in junk shops and at auctions. By the end of the century the Gustav Becker factory had amalgamated with other firms in the area to become the United Freiburg Clock Factories, to compete with similar large concerns which had begun to appear in the Black Forest owned by firms such as Junghans, Kienzle, the Hamburg American Clock Company (set up, as the name suggests, to produce German versions of American clocks) and Winterhalder & Hofmeier. These companies, and others in the Black Forest, produced and exported clocks in large quantities.

Nowadays there is still a considerable clockmaking industry in Germany, though most of the clocks being produced have quartz movements. That said, mechanical cuckoo clocks retain much of their popularity and are still being made, as are 400-day clocks – though the numbers of these with true mechanical movements are declining. The firm of Kieninger still produces a variety of different mechanical movements in Aldingen, as well as complete clocks in the regulator style.

plain rectangular wooden cases, perhaps with a simple cresting top and bottom and a square window below the dial through which the movement of the pendulum could be viewed.

While the Black Forest was the main production center for clocks in Germany, there were others, particularly Freiburg in Silesia, where in 1850 an Austrian-trained clockmaker, Gustav Becker, set up a factory to produce clocks similar to the Vienna regulators which he had

CHAPTER 8

Clocks for the wall

WALL-HANGING CLOCKS have been popular since the earliest days of domestic horology. In France, for example, the cartel clock became popular during the eighteenth century, and in Germany the wall clock became a mainstay of the Black Forest clockmaking industry in the latter part of the nineteenth century. Wall clocks were also made in some numbers in other parts of Europe – particularly Austria – and in America, where elegant and expensive wall clocks were designed and built by Simon Willard, Lemuel Curtis and others. In Britain, too, wall clocks evolved a style peculiar to their type, particularly the 'Act of Parliament' or 'tavern' clock and the ubiquitous 'English dial'.

In 1797 the British Parliament passed an Act which levied a tax of five shillings per annum on all clocks and ten shillings on gold watches. As a result of this, the story goes, people began to get rid of their domestic timekeepers, relying instead on clocks in public places such as coaching inns etc. The story goes on to conclude that the so-called Act of Parliament clock was developed as a result of this legislation, hence the name. In fact there is no evidence to suggest that this is actually what happened, and the tavern clock in any case is known to have existed in the early part of the eighteenth century, well before the enactment of this particular piece of legislation.

Tavern clocks are very distinctive in appearance. The typical example has a case made entirely of wood. Even the dial is of wood, often lacquered black, with the hour numbers applied in gilt and gold leaf and with no glass to cover them. The dials of tavern clocks were big and bold, enabling them to be seen even in dimly lit, smoke-filled bars. The dial might be squared off at the bottom, with an arched top and 'ear pieces' applied where the bottom of the dial meets the drop trunk in which the pendulum swings. Alternatively a good number of early tavern clocks had octagonal dials. The trunk or back box – often referred to as the 'salt box' – extends below the dial, the front of which is often decorated with oriental type lacquerwork and the maker's name and location. It has a shaped base and a door at the front to allow the pendulum to be adjusted.

A French cartel clock. c.1745. The case was made by Charles Cressent of Paris, a prominent bronze worker of his day, and the movement by Guiot.

A round-dial tavern or 'Act of Parliament' clock by William Nash of Bridge (Canterbury) who died in 1794. This imposing clock is five feet tall.

81

LEFT
'Teardrop'-cased tavern clock by Philip
Lloyd of Bristol, c.1780.

*RIGHT
Mahogany-cased white dial tavern
clock by Matthew Worgan of Bristol
dating from the end of the eighteenth
century.*

Tavern clock movements are simple in construction, these clocks normally being simple timekeepers without strike or chime, and changing little during the century of tavern clock manufacture. The plates were tapered, being narrower at the top than at the bottom, possibly in an effort to use less brass. The clocks are normally weight-driven – occasionally spring-driven – with a train of four or five wheels and an anchor escapement. Typically tavern clocks run for a week at one winding. Occasionally these clocks may be encountered with 'passing strike', striking a single blow at the hour, and even less often with full striking, sounding one blow at one o'clock, two at two o'clock and so on up the twelve. Around the middle of the eighteenth century tavern clocks with circular black dials began to make their appearance, these being fairly quickly superseded by white circular dials, the clocks now beginning to resemble the English dial, though the two styles are now thought to have followed separate lines of evolution.

The English dial is the traditional wooden-cased

'office' or 'schoolroom' clock of the nineteenth and early twentieth centuries, though it first appeared towards the end of the eighteenth century. It is thought to have evolved from the 'cartel' clock, an ornate brass and gilt wood wall clock made in France and then Britain in the early part of the eighteenth century. The English dial clock is essentially an English cartel clock with a plain wooden case: the movement and dial are those of the earlier style, but the case consists simply of a circular wooden dial surround and a salt box back, most often not projecting below the movement and being hidden completely, from the front view, by the dial surround. As the style progressed, English dials appeared with octagonal surrounds and with trunks which extended below the dial, the latter now being known as 'drop dials'.

While early English dial clocks had small dials of about nine inches in diameter made from silvered brass, these were quickly superseded by clocks with twelve inch white wooden dials, convex in shape and with black painted numerals. These wooden dials were in turn replaced by white painted iron dials, again usually convex in shape, and later still by flat painted white dials. Unlike tavern clocks, early English dials had verge escapements and short bob pendulums, the verge escapement being replaced after a few decades by the more reliable anchor. The movement plates of early English dials had a similar tapered shape to those of the tavern clock, and they were normally made without strike. One major difference from the tavern clock, however, was that the English dials were all spring-driven.

These clocks, the most popular type of mechanical clock ever made, were still in production as late as the 1930s, when they were superseded by synchronous wall

LEFT
Early English dial clock, c.1820 by Cohen of Hastings. The dial is of painted wood and the bezel of cast brass.

ABOVE
The motive force for this gravity clock is provided by its own weight, as the force of gravity pulls it down a toothed rack.

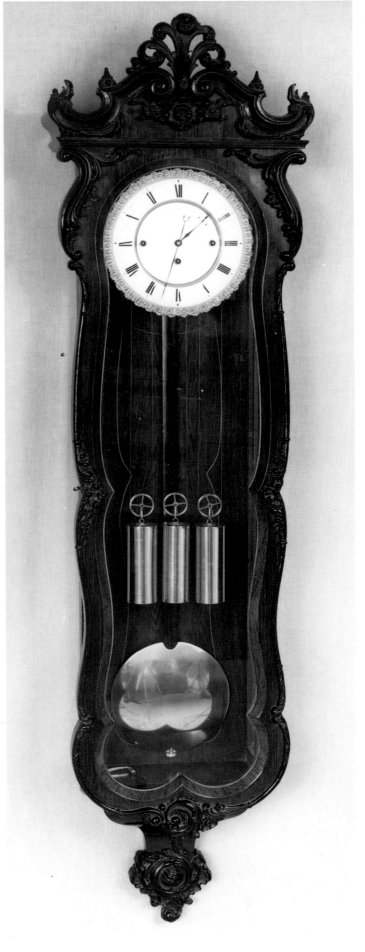

84

clocks and master-and-slave systems, both of which had the advantage of not needing to be wound. Clocks similar in style to the English dial were manufactured as far afield as the USA. Their simple, unfussy lines fit in well with modern decor and they are becoming collectable in their own right.

The same is true of another type of European wall clock, the Vienna regulator, which until recently was overlooked by collectors but is now finding great popularity both as a horological type and as a furnishing item. The name is rather misleading, as this clock was not in the strict sense a regulator - and was in fact made by clock-makers throughout Austria and Hungary during the nineteenth century. These Vienna wall clocks, as they are also called, have precision pendulum controlled movements, normally weight driven, often with striking and chiming trains. They are housed in elegant wooden cases, with glazed front and sides which allow the weights and pendulum to be seen, adding considerably to the visual effect. The pendulum rod is normally of black painted wood – occasionally of steel – and terminates in a large and highly polished brass-cased bob. The weights hang on pulleys directly below the movement and, like the bob, are cased in highly polished brass. The movement itself is of delicate high-quality construction, with dead-beat escapement, finely cut teeth and narrow pivots, and is mounted on the back board of the case via substantial cast-iron brackets. While most Vienna wall clocks were built to run for eight days, examples exist of month, three-month and year duration.

The Vienna wall clock first appeared in the early part of the nineteenth century during the 'Empire' period. Early examples were similar in appearance to the floor-standing longcase clocks from which they had evolved, with a distinct hood (usually with an architectural or 'roof-top' pediment), trunk and base. These early Viennas were known as 'laterndluhr' or 'lantern clocks' because the glazed cases resembled lanterns. The pendulum rod of lanterndluhrs is often of steel rather than wood, and these clocks have white or silvered dials.

The Empire period was followed, around 1820, by the Biedermeier Period, and Vienna wall clocks became more ornate. Cases had scrolled carvings at the top and bottom, and were now more in the shape of a straight rectangle, with no separate hood and base; the bottom of the case was often shaped to resemble a wall bracket.

The Neoclassical Period, the last years, of the true Vienna wall clock, began around 1850 and lasted until nearly the end of the century, by which time these high-quality precision timekeepers were being superseded by cheaper clocks in a similar style produced in clock-making factories across the border in Germany. While the movements of these Neoclassical Viennas did not differ substantially from those of the earlier periods, the cases tended to be elaborately decorated with classical motifs, though during this period cheaper Vienna wall clocks were also being made with simple time-only

LEFT
A rosewood Vienna regulator with grande sonnerie striking on two gongs, c.1855.

BELOW
American drop dial wall clock, c.1870, by Atkins Clock Co. of Bristol Connecticut.

FAR LEFT
A single-weight Vienna regulator, c.1825, in a plain roof-top case.

LEFT
A miniature German wall regulator, c.1900. The pendulum bob of this clock carries the letters 'R/A', for 'retard' and 'advance'.

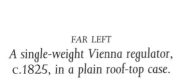

movements in plain cases to compete with the products flooding in from the German factories.

The German clockmaking industry, as we have seen, became industrialized in the middle of the nineteenth century. It was then able to produce clocks cheaply as long as it could sell them in quantity, and as a result the owners of German clock factories began to look out-wards to find international markets for their products. German-made versions of Vienna wall clocks are generally of reasonable quality, though lacking the finely finished precision movements of their Austrian counter-parts. While early examples had a close visual resem-blance to the Viennas from which they were evolving, in later years the cases became much simpler and more aus-tere, often little more than a rectangular wooden box with a glazed front, straight hands and a shaped top. These clocks were still being made well into the twen-tieth century – both in Germany and, by then, in the USA.

In America, clockmakers were also making wall clocks in their own highly distinctive styles, the princes among these being the 'banjo' and its derivative the 'girandole'. The banjo, patented in 1802, just a couple of decades after the signing of the Declaration of Independence, was one of the first clocks which was truly American in style, and many of its features have appeared in later, factory-made American clocks. Some claim that the design was based on the Act of Parliament clock, but this appears to be un-substantiated. The banjo is in fact more likely to have been derived from the 'gallery' clocks which were then being used to show the time in public buildings in the United States.

The idea of the banjo clock which, as the name sug-gests, was vaguely similar to a banjo in shape, was first conceived by Simon Willard of Roxbury, Massachussetts. The name was coined later. The case of the banjo consists of three parts: the upper dial portion, behind which the movement is mounted, a tapered middle portion in which the weight falls and a rectangular box at the bot-tom which allows for the swing of the pendulum bob. Both the middle portion and the box have often elaborately painted glass fronts.

The eight-day weight-driven movement of the banjo was unusual at the time in two respects. First, the pendu-lum swung in front of the movement rather than behind it, with a stirrup on the crutch to allow it to clear the hour and minute hand extensions. Second, the barrel was mounted close to the two o'clock position to allow an extra inch or two fall for the weights.

Willard's design was a great success with the clock-buying public in America and his design was copied by many of his contemporaries. A later variation had the center portion in the shape of a lyre, and later still another variant was developed by Lemuel Curtis of Concord, Massachussetts, with a circular base and more elaborate decoration. Both the banjos of Simon Willard and the girandoles of Lemuel Curtis are extremely rare and very highly prized by American clock collectors.

Two Vienna wall clocks by W Schonberger of Vienna. That on the left dating from 1845 is unusual in having spring-driven grande sonnerie striking though the going train is weight driven. The clock on the right, c.1860, runs for three months at a single winding.

LEFT
A Simon Willard 'banjo' clock, highly prized by clock collectors in the US. Note the winding square close to the two o'clock position. This allows an extra few inches fall for the extra weights, helping to ensure that the clock will run for a full eight days.

CHAPTER 9

The Skeleton Clock

ALL CLOCKS have visual appeal. The shape of the case, the engraving on the dial, the motion of the hands, the movement of the pendulum – all these enhance the attraction of what is essentially a functional instrument. Perhaps the most visually appealing clock of all is one which has no case, which often has a delicately pierced dial, and one in which the movement plates are shaped in a fantastic variety of forms. This is the skeleton clock.

The skeleton clock differs from most other clock types in having a movement which is entirely visible. The movement – in English terms similar to the movement of a bracket clock or a dial clock, but better finished – has been, as the name suggests, reduced to a mere 'skeleton', the plates, back and front, have been pierced, fretted and shaped in a variety of styles to enhance the visual attractiveness of what would otherwise be plain brass plates. The dial too, particularly in English clocks, is often fretted out. One further effect of this 'skeletonization' is that the wheels and escapement of the clock become visible – all the moving parts can be freely observed – enhancing still further the visual appeal of this type of clock. Skeleton clocks have no case; they are generally mounted on a base of marble or wood and covered by a glass dome or 'shade' to protect the movement from dust and to minimize tarnishing.

Many skeleton clocks were mass produced by companies such as Smiths of Clerkenwell and Evans of Handsworth. Typically these are simple timekeepers or have only 'passing strike', where the clocks strikes a single blow each hour. Skeleton clocks, often showing no clockmaker's name, can be very difficult to date. Styles did not change a great deal over the years and even modern skeleton clocks made from kits have a strong superficial resemblance to Victorian examples. Others, however, are elaborate and elegant structures. Here you may find wheels which are delicately cut, elaborations of the movement to include calendar work and chiming, and unusual and visually attractive escapements. Such clocks are the work of makers anxious to show off their skills to maximum effect.

ABOVE
A complex skeleton clock, c.1790 made for the French market and signed 'Martinet, London'.

RIGHT
An English skeleton clock, c.1865, inspired by the onion-shaped dome of Brighton Pavilion. This clock was made by Smiths of Clerkenwell, London.

In more recent years watches have appeared with skeletonized movements and abbreviated dials, allowing the fast-moving escape wheel to be seen through the watch glass. These are very attractive specimens, though the dials are often very difficult to read.

Though the first skeleton clocks are thought to have been made in France around the middle of the eighteenth century – and while skeleton clocks were produced, as we shall see, in continental Europe and even in the United States – the style is often considered to have reached its fullest flowering among the fads and fashions of Victorian Britain.

The early English skeletons – generally simple timepieces with no striking or chiming – had a similar overall appearance to the continental skeleton clocks from which they had evolved, but the English quickly developed a style of their own, based on 'A'-shaped plates or 'frames' decorated with scrolls and curlicues and housing a single train spring-and-fusee driven movement, often with passing strike. The English skeleton became more elaborate throughout the nineteenth century, both in terms of movement complexity and frame design. Clockmakers used skeletons to demonstrate how well they could make a new type of escapement. They installed proper striking, chiming and even music work. And they constructed frames which resembled famous buildings such as York Minster or the Scott Monument.

In the latter half of the nineteenth century, the style reached its peak, and skeleton clocks were being produced by the thousand throughout the country. But

LEFT
A Victorian brass chiming skeleton clock based on the architecture of York Minster Cathedral.

RIGHT
A simple time-only fusee-driven English skeleton clock.

towards the end of the century – faced with increasing competition from factories like Smiths of Clerkenwell and with imports of cheap mass-produced clocks from Germany, France and the United States – the traditional British clockmaking industry fell into decline. Skeleton clocks were to be mass-produced as parts of standard ranges. These skeletons were sold on to retailers who were then free to put their own names on the clocks.

By the end of the century, in any case, the style was going out of fashion. Skeleton clocks were no longer popular with the general public, and production declined – though it never entirely ceased. Skeleton clocks can still be found which were made in the distinctive styles of the 1920s and 1930s.

In more recent years, the British skeleton clock has regained some of the popularity that it lost as the world moved into a new – and less fussy – age at the beginning of the twentieth century. Modern clockmakers have published details and plans which allow the constructional enthusiast to make his or her own skeleton clock in the home workshop; kits are available to make this process easier.

In France, where the style originated, skeleton clocks were elegant instruments, often with extremely large and delicate wheels, with 300 or more teeth on the largest or

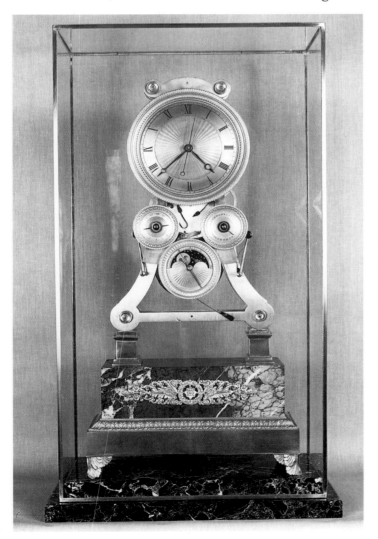

LEFT
French 'Great Exhibition' skeleton clock, so called because this type was first seen at the Great Exhibition in London, 1851.

BELOW FAR LEFT
A complex skeleton clock by the French clockmaker Verneuil, who seems to have specialized in clocks of this type.

BELOW LEFT
A Victorian 'great wheel' skeleton clock by the famous Liverpool clockmaker James Condliff. The mainspring is mounted within the wooden base.

RIGHT
French 'great wheel' skeleton. The largest wheels of clocks of this type have several hundred teeth.

LEFT
A striking weight-driven skeleton by the American Aaron Dodd Crane. The three balls in the base of this clock are the 'bob' of Crane's torsion pendulum.

RIGHT
Many skeleton clocks, like this one, were built with an inverted 'Y'-shaped frame.

'great' wheel. Because of the size of the great wheel – and other wheels in the train – these clocks required fewer wheels than their English counterparts. Great wheel clocks often had a single wheel between the great wheel, which was driven directly by the going barrel, and the escape wheel. This intermediate wheel was normally concentric with, and very slightly larger than, the chapter ring, enhancing still further the stunning simplicity of these elegant timekeepers.

The wheels of these clocks are often mounted between plates in the shape of an inverted 'Y', or sometimes on a glass plate which allows the entire workings of the clock

BELOW
An 'epicyclic' skeleton clock, so-called because it uses epicyclic gearing where one wheel revolves around a fixed wheel. This type was invented by William Strutt and put into production by his friend William Wigston of Derby.

RIGHT
An ornate mid-nineteenth century Viennese skeleton clock which incorporates grande sonnerie striking.

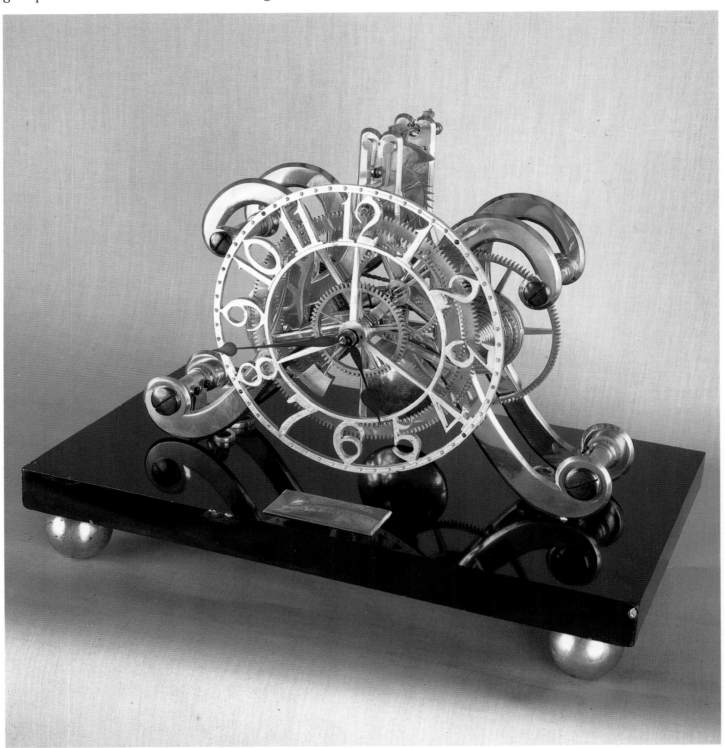

to be viewed from front or rear. Like their English counterparts, most French skeleton clocks are spring-driven, though in most cases the great wheel is attached directly to the spring barrel, rather than being driven via a chain and fusee. Weight-driven examples do exist, the weights normally being suspended on pulley arrangements either side of the movement, but these are rather ponderous affairs, lacking much of the beauty of spring-driven clocks.

One prominent feature of many French skeleton clocks is their astonishing complexity. French makers seem to have been keen to cram as many features as possible into a single skeletonized movement and as a result many French skeletons are an impressive – if bewildering – display of the clockmaker's art. Often these clocks run for a month or even a year, and incorporate seconds indication, calendar-work, moon-work, equation of time, music-work and more, displaying these functions on a multiplicity of subsidiary dials.

In Austria, the skeleton clock often consisted of a circular movement supported by two pillars, between which hung a decorative pendulum, the whole standing on a circular or oval base. Austrian skeleton clocks are often ornately decorated and often weight driven, the weights hanging from pulleys directly beneath the movement.

In the United States, the vast majority of clock movements were skeletonized. Raw materials such as brass were scarce and hence any unnecessary brass was fretted out of the plates for recycling. These movements, however, were normally housed in wooden cases and they cannot be considered as true skeleton clocks, where the plates are skeletonized in order that the movement should be more fully displayed.

It should also be noted that by the time the skeleton clock achieved its peak of popularity in fashion-conscious Europe, the American clockmaking industry was already well advanced in terms of organizing itself into factories, mass-producing clocks on a production line basis. The individual American clockmaker disappeared long before his counterparts in England.

Nevertheless, there were skilled individual craftsmen making clocks in America anxious, like European clockmakers, to show off their skills to greatest advantage. Makers such as Aaron D Crane, inventor of the torsion pendulum, produced some ingenious and elegant designs. However this was the exception rather than the rule. Though records exist of one or two skeleton clocks which went into mass production in the United States, the skeleton clock style does not appear to have taken hold of the buying public's imagination in America in the way it did in England, France and Austria.

An account of skeleton clock development – especially at the more complex end of the spectrum – would hardly be complete without mention of the 'orrery', a complex instrument often driven or controlled by a skeletonized clock movement and incorporating a clock dial which shows the relative sizes and positions of the planets in the solar system. The first orrery was made for Charles Boyle, fourth Earl of Orrery, by the English clockmaker John Rowley, though the design appears to have been copied from an earlier instrument devised by George Graham. Soon these complex instruments became fashionable and were to be found as conversation pieces in stately homes the length and breadth of England. In France Antide Janvier and his apprentice Raingo experimented with orreries – one particular type of clock-orrery now bears Raingo's name – as did a number of other French makers. In more recent years, a number of craftsman-clockmakers in Britain and elsewhere have built orreries as exhibition pieces.

BELOW
A nineteenth century English Gothic-style skeleton clock with passing strike.

RIGHT
A skeletonized French clock orrery with a glass star globe c.1800.

CHAPTER 10

Novelty Clocks

THERE IS something about the clock and its movement which induces people to manufacture unusual and in some cases downright peculiar variants of it. This may be a result of the desire to use new materials and more economic production methods. It may be an attempt to enhance the aesthetic appeal of the clock. Or it may be an attempt by the clockmaker to improve on some technical aspect. For whatever reason, there is no doubt that over the centuries clockmakers throughout the world have produced an immense variety of types of clock, many of the more unusual of which are now referred to as 'novelty' clocks.

We have already seen how the skeleton clock achieved great popularity throughout Europe in the nineteenth century, yet the idea of exposing and enhancing a clock movement was originally a novelty. Early skeleton clocks were thus undoubtedly novelty clocks, though their subsequent popularity has moved them into mainstream horology. Perhaps the best-known type of horological novelty is the 'mystery' clock or, as the French know it, the *mysterieuse*. The mystery here is that there is no visible means of keeping the pendulum swinging or of propelling the hands, which appear to move independently, with no apparent connection to anything resembling a movement.

Mystery clocks are thought to have originated in France or Germany, probably in the seventeenth century. It was not until the nineteenth century, however, that the idea was taken up enthusiastically by French clockmakers and mystery clocks were produced in some numbers. More recently they have been produced and marketed in a variety of exotic forms by exclusive stores such as Aspreys and Cartier of London.

One of the most amusing and intriguing forms of mysterieuse is the 'tortoise' or 'turtle' clock, so called because it features a small turtle or tortoise floating in a shallow circular pool of water, around the edges of which are inscribed the hours of the day. As if by magic the turtle 'swims' around the edge of the pool at a rate corresponding to the passage of time, marking the hours as it

LEFT
A French mystery clock. The movement is housed in the sphere behind the clock dial. The whole clock/pendulum assembly rocks to and fro in the hand of the female statuette with no apparent force of motive power.

ABOVE
A group of three French mystery clocks. The clocks to the left and right, where the hands have no apparent connection to the movement in the base, are by Robert Houdin. The clock in the center indicates time by the rising and falling of the hands of the female figurine.

RIGHT
A tortoise clock. The turtle or tortoise in the pool of water moves round the clock dial under the influence of a magnet in the base of the clock.

LEFT
*Organ clocks like this were a
popular, if expensive type of
novelty in Europe.*

BELOW
*A magnificent nineteenth century
French mystery clock in ormolu.*

moves. Even if the turtle is deliberately moved away from its correct position, it will slowly swim back.

The secret here lies in the fact that there is a clock movement concealed just below the bottom of the pool which drives a magnetic hour hand. The turtle, made mainly of wood, incorporates a small piece of iron which causes it to be attracted to the magnetic hand, and thus it moves round the dial at a rate corresponding to the movement of the hand, keeping the correct time as it goes.

Another popular form of mystery clock has a transparent glass dial on which is affixed a single hour hand. There is no apparent movement and nothing – as far as one can see – driving the hand. Yet it slowly moves round the dial keeping the correct time. In reality the dial is made of two circular sheets of glass sandwiched together, the hand being mounted on one sheet, the dial markings on the other. The glass disc which carries the hands has teeth cut into its edge – which are concealed by a brass rim – and these are driven from a movement in the base of the clock. Because the glass is transparent, only the hand seems to move.

One of the most intriguing mystery clocks of all was the 'mysterious circulator' invented and patented in 1808 by John Schmidt, a Dutchman working in London. In Schmidt's clock the single hour hand was freely pivoted in the center of the chapter ring – it could be moved simply by blowing on it – yet, mysteriously, it slowly moved around the dial to show the correct time. Even if someone deliberately interfered with it, it would return automatically to display the correct time. The hand was delicately counterbalanced by a weight attached to a tiny watch movement hidden behind its non-pointing end. When the watch movement was wound up, the weight slowly moved round, causing the other end of the hand to indicate the correct time on the clock dial.

Perhaps the most popular type of mystery clock of all was one produced first in France, and then America, towards the end of the nineteenth century – the so-called 'Swinging Diana' or 'Diana Swinger'. Here a statuette, often resembling the mythological goddess Diana, holds a rod in her outstretched hand, with a clock dial at the upper end and a pendulum bob at the lower. The rod swings slowly back and forth, pivoted in the hand of the statuette, and the clock keeps time. These are spring driven clocks, with the movement behind the clock dial at the upper end of the rod. The rod acts as a pendulum and a small weight inside the clock movement trips the escapement as it swings. The weight then moves in the opposite direction, impulsing the pendulum as it does so.

Another popular type of horological novelty was the moving figure or 'automaton', the earliest known of which was part of the famous Strasbourg clock, completed in the 1320s. Besides displaying the time, this showed the movements of the planets and incorporated a figure of a cock which, on the stroke of twelve, opened

its beak, stuck out its tongue, 'crowed' and flapped its wings.

Ever since this early experiment, automata have been a popular horological extra, clockmakers using a variety of ingenious mechanisms to make the figures move. Many early German clocks featured automata, often with a religious theme – the twelve apostles appearing before the figure of Christ, for example, or the three kings before the Madonna and baby Jesus. Early public clocks – such as the famous clock in St Marks Square, Venice – often had figures which struck, or appeared to strike, the hours on a bell or bells. In the eighteenth and nineteenth centuries,

ABOVE
An Austrian or Swiss automaton table clock with organ. This clock is in a walnut and parquetry case with applied decoration in ormolu. It dates from the Biedermeier Period (1825-50).

RIGHT
A pair of 'swinging ball' mystery clocks.

English longcases often had automata in the dial arch, rocking ships and moving eyes being popular themes.

In more recent years, elaborate automata have become a popular feature of clocks in shopping centers, parks and other public places. One splendid example of this type of clock was built in a public park in Norwich, England, in the mid-1980s. This clock, known as the Gurney clock after a prominent Norwich banking family, has a lion automaton which picks up a golden ball with its paw and moves it to another location in the clock. This is accompanied by a series of movements which see the ball being moved through a wonderland scenario in which a castle and the lion represent the city of Norwich and a set of scales represents the bank.

Some novelty clocks use unusual escapements as the basis of their novelty. One such is the Congreve clock, named after its inventor William Congreve, who patented his design at the beginning of the nineteenth century. Congreve, later Sir William Congreve, went on to become equerry to the Prince Regent and Comptroller of the Royal Laboratory at Woolwich Arsenal.

The Congreve clock has an escapement consisting of a metal table with a zig-zag groove cut into its surface in which runs a small steel ball. The table is pivoted at its center and when the clock is going it rocks slowly from one side to the other. As it does so, the ball runs down the zig-zag groove to what is now the lower end of the table. Here it moves a lever which causes the platform to tilt the other way and at the same time triggers the escapement. The ball now runs back along the zig-zag track to trigger a lever at the other end and the whole process begins again.

Congreve clocks are usually spring-driven and show the hours and minutes on separate dials. Though they are

RIGHT
A 'Congreve' or 'rolling ball'
clock invented by Sir William
Congreve, Comptroller of the
Royal Laboratory at Woolwich
Arsenal, 1808. Here the
escapement is controlled by a
small steel ball rolling along a
series of zig-zag channels on a
tilting plate mounted below the
movement.

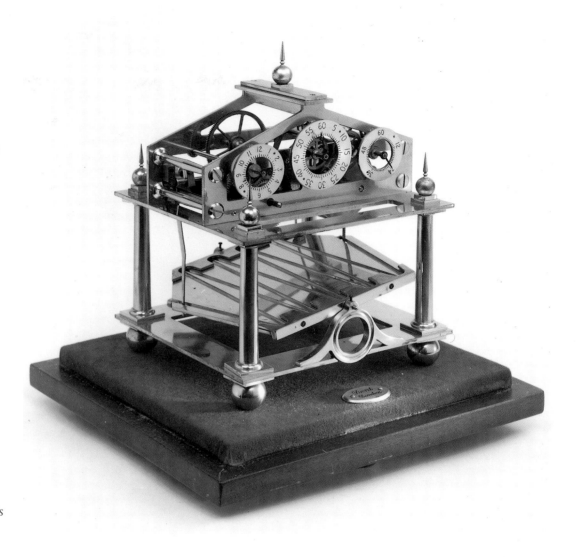

LEFT
A Viennese automaton picture
clock, c.1805. When the hour is
struck, the figures and devices
begin to move.

poor timekeepers – and noisy in operation – these clocks have maintained a certain level of popularity since their invention due to their novelty appeal. Congreve presented his first clock to the Prince Regent. It is now in the Rotunda at Woolwich, London.

The flying pendulum (or flying ball) clock was another in which the action of an unusual – and highly entertaining – escapement gave it a great market appeal. The movement of this clock is mounted in a rectangular box, through the top of which protrudes an extension of the arbor of what would normally be the escape wheel. This carries a length of cotton thread, to the other end of which is attached a small metal ball. As the arbor revolves, the ball swings round on the end of the thread until the thread comes into contact with one of a pair of posts mounted on top of the box on either side of the extended arbor. The momentum of the ball causes the thread to wrap itself round the post and when this has happened the weight of the ball causes it to unwind. The arbor is then free to swing round again until the thread comes into contact with the post opposite, and the whole process is repeated. Like the Congreve, the flying pendulum clock is a poor timekeeper which has recently come back

into vogue as a conversation piece.

The novelty of the 400-day clock is, as the name suggests, that it will run for over a year at a single winding. This type of clock also uses a novel type of escapement controlled by a 'torsion' pendulum, which revolves slowly on its own axis, first in one direction, then in the other. It is this very efficient escapement which allows the clock to run for such a long period of time.

The torsion pendulum was devised in 1829 by the American clockmaking genius Aaron Dodd Crane, though 50 years were to pass before a similar type of escapement devised by the German Anton Harder was to become the basis of commercially produced 400-day clocks. These became popular gifts for US servicemen in Europe to send home to their wives on anniversaries, hence their American name 'Anniversary clocks'.

The pendulum of early 400-day clocks was a flat disc of brass. Later models featured ornamental lead-filled brass balls which could be moved in or out to regulate the timekeeping. The clocks have enjoyed great popularity throughout the twentieth century and is still being produced today – though most of the clocks now being sold with what appear to be torsion pendulums have quartz

107

ABOVE
The 'Kee-Less' gravity clock uses its own weight as its motive power. It is wound up by being moved to the top of the two supports and as it runs, it gradually moves down.

LEFT
This 400-day or 'Anniversary' clock, c.1905, uses a special torsion pendulum to allow it to run for an entire year at a single winding. Early models like this used a flat cylindrical weight as the pendulum bob.

RIGHT
Later 400-day clocks used decorative brass balls for the pendulum bob. These can be moved in and out to regulate timekeeping.

movements and the pendulums are purely cosmetic, playing no role in timekeeping.

Another German clock which surely qualifies as a novelty is the cuckoo clock, so often – and wrongly – attributed to the Swiss. Credit for the invention of this type of clock is usually given to Franz Anton Ketterer, one of the earliest known clockmakers in the Black Forest, and the first cuckoo clocks are said to date from around 1730.

Early cuckoo clocks are thought merely to have imitated the sound of the bird after which they are named and to have been made in the style of popular clocks of the day. The painted wooden cuckoo which popped out when the hours were sounded was a later development. The style of cuckoo clock which became popular as a parlour decoration in the twentieth century – a small house or 'chalet' decorated with ornate and elaborate carving – is thought to have been developed in the closing years of the nineteenth century. The original cuckoo clocks were driven by weights in the shape of elongated pine cones; later models were spring driven.

Over the 400 or so years of domestic mechanical horology a great number of other kinds of novelty clocks have been devised and constructed. Clocks were produced, for example, which used their own weight as the motive force, gradually descending down a toothed rod or rack. Clocks were built into landscape pictures, often showing a village dominated by a clock tower, with the clock actually showing the correct time. Public clocks were built with dials mounted in flower beds – the famous floral clock in Edinburgh being an excellent example. Many more types of novelty clock are also to be found.

LEFT
A tripod clock by Thomas Cole, a variant of this famous maker's well-known 'strut' clock.

RIGHT
Early cuckoo clocks were based on
contemporary clock designs,
rather than on the carved chalets
that we see today.

ABOVE

A night clock which used electric light to project the time display to the ceiling at night.

LEFT

A 'blinking eye' clock, c.1860. In this popular novelty clock, the figure moves its eyes or blinks as the clock ticks.

RIGHT

Though not strictly in the novelty category, Japanese clocks like this unusual sculptural model are extremely uncommon in the West. Japan used a system of 'unequal hours' until 1873, dividing each day into six hours of daylight and six hours of darkness. As the lengths of night and day vary throughout the year, Japanese clocks had movable hour indicators.

CHAPTER 11

Watches

THE FIRST clocks were massive and crude, wrought from iron by the blacksmith at his forge using heavy tools and lacking both hands and dials. Centuries passed before clocks were produced that were small enough for domestic use. Soon after the appearance of the first domestic timekeepers, there was a development that was slowly to revolutionize the world of mechanical horology, to allow the production of clocks which were truly portable, and ultimately at the peak of miniaturization, the manufacture of watches small enough to be carried in the waistcoat pocket and even worn on the wrist. That development was the production of mainsprings reliable enough to be used as the driving force for mechanical timekeepers.

Early watches, like early clocks, incorporated a verge escapement and were not reliable enough to merit a minute hand, far less a seconds hand. Around 1675, however, the balance spring made its appearance courtesy

of Dutch scientist Christiaan Huygens. This invention was as significant in its own way as the introduction (again by Huygens) of the pendulum in clocks, and gave watches a degree of reliability hitherto unthinkable. It was now possible to adjust watch escapements and ensured that the watches of the future would be useful timekeeping instruments rather than just the playthings of rich and influential men.

Many verge watches still exist, often achieving high prices at auction. They can be recognized by their cases which are thicker than those of later pocket watches, and by the ornate decoration of both the cases and the movements, showing perhaps that the other prime function of these watches – besides their use as timekeepers – was as elaborately chased and engraved pieces of jewelry. The balance cock, in fact, would often incorporate a large cut diamond as endstone to the balance staff.

LEFT
English verge escapement pocket watch by Edward Wrench of Chelsea. This watch is housed in a silver 'pair' case – the watch movement is contained in an inner case and this is afforded further protection by a second outer case.

RIGHT
A group of sixteenth century verge pocket watches showing the movements.

THIS PAGE
Seventeenth century verge pocket
watch movements showing elaborately
engraved and pierced balance wheel
cocks.

RIGHT
This verge pocket watch strikes the hours and repeats the striking at will. Note the intricately pierced hands. This watch was exquisitely recased during the decade 1740-1750 (below).

LEFT
*Watches came in as great a
variety of styles in the seventeenth
century as they do today.*

A group of seventeenth century pocket watches showing intricate decoration typical of the period.

ABOVE
George I gold pocket watch by the famous George Graham of London.

LEFT
Bold-cased English lever pocket watch signed 'R & G Beesley, Liverpool'. Richard and George Beesley are known to have been active in the first half of the nineteenth century.

RIGHT
Movement of pocket watch using English lever escapement and cut bimetallic balance for temperature compensation.

ABOVE
Another George I gold pocket watch by Graham. Note similarities with Graham watch shown opposite.

Many developments followed which influenced the evolution of the watch. One was the use of the fusee in watches, already used in clocks to equalize the power supplied to the escapement as the mainspring ran down. Another was the pioneering work of John Harrison, who, as we have seen, developed timekeepers which would keep time accurately even aboard a ship being pitched from side to side in a storm. Two further developments which had a major impact on watches were the invention of the cylinder escapement by Tompion, Booth and Houghton at the end of the seventeenth century and the invention of the lever escapement in the middle of the eighteenth century, now generally attributed to the English horologist Thomas Mudge. These introduced a new degree of accuracy into watches and allowed the movements to be slimmer and lighter.

Over the years lever escapement watches were produced in vast numbers, particularly in England, Switzerland and, later on, in the United States. The cylinder escapement, cheaper to produce than the lever but slightly less accurate, enjoyed currency in Switzerland until the middle of the nineteenth century when it began to fall from favor, to be replaced by the lever.

Once fully evolved, the lever escapement existed in two forms, now known as the 'English lever' and the 'Swiss lever'. The English lever had pallets, generally of steel, mounted in line with the body of the lever. The Swiss version, on the other hand, had the pallets mounted on arms projecting from either side of one end of the lever.

Early watches, like early clocks, were made more or less from scratch by a single craftsman, a skilled technician who cut and shaped all of the parts, assembled them into a movement, and finally finished, timed and adjusted the watch. As the Industrial Revolution swept Europe, however, leaving behind it a much larger and more affluent middle class, demand for watches rose spectacularly. Towards the end of the eighteenth century, the watchmaking trade in England began to diversify, taking on the nature of a 'cottage industry', using semi-skilled outworkers in their homes to make the individual parts of a movement, these being simply assembled and adjusted by a 'finisher' and finally sold by the retailer or 'watchmaker' whose name appeared on the movement and dial of the finished watch. Thus a fusee-cutter made the fusee, a chain-maker the fusee chain, a hand-maker the hands, and a wheel-cutter the wheels. In all, some 20 different individuals might be involved in the watch manufacturing process, each making different parts of the movement, the whole process being co-ordinated and controlled by the retailer. The movements, or 'ebauches', of English watches were often made in the provinces, notably Coventry and Prescot, Lancashire.

In Switzerland, the craft of watchmaking developed in a radically different way. While at the beginning of the nineteenth century Swiss watchmaking was organized on much the same cottage-industry basis as the English watch trade, in the years which followed the workers who made the parts of the watch movements began to move into factories; the whole manufacturing process

LEFT
Movement of striking and repeating verge watch dating from the early eighteenth century.

OVERLEAF
Group of 'keyless' lever pocket watches, and opposite, their movements. These are wound by turning the 'crown' inside the pendant.

THIS PAGE
A selection of gold pocket and fob watches from Switzerland. These use the ubiquitous Swiss lever escapement, which became the standard for mechanical wristwatches in the twentieth century.

BELOW
A group of eighteenth century pocket watches. The watch in the lower left-hand corner has an unusual type of calendar indication while the watch beside it has a 'Turkish' style dial.

RIGHT
Ladies gold watch dating from the end of the nineteenth century made by the highly successful American Waltham Watch company of Waltham, Massachussetts.

was centralized and, more importantly, standardized. Mass-production techniques were introduced. Now parts – screws, wheels, escapements – were made in huge numbers and could be used in a whole variety of different movements, allowing economies of scale to bring production costs down. Sophisticated machines began to be used in the manufacture of watch parts, allowing greater precision and accuracy in the manufacturing process. As a result of the move to mass production, Swiss factories needed mass markets, and so began aggressively marketing and exporting their products throughout Europe and the rest of the world. Faced with this competition – in a market flooded with watches which were both cheaper and more accurate – the English watch trade, still organized as a cottage industry, went into terminal decline.

There was one notable – but in the end unsuccessful – attempt to reverse this decline, to set up a factory-based watch manufacturing system in England and beat the Swiss predators at their own game. The Lancashire Watch

Company (LWC) was established in 1888 and though it lasted only until 1910, it produced hundreds of thousands of watches. At its peak 1000 workers were manufacturing 2000 watches a week. Many of these watches – in a great variety – are still to be found at fleamarkets and antique fairs in the UK. Watches and movements are displayed in the Prescot Museum, Prescot, Lancashire.

The failure of the Lancashire Watch Company to match the successes of its Swiss competitors has been debated at great length in horological circles. One possible reason often put forward is that many of the company's employees, formerly self-employed in making parts for watch finishers, were half-hearted about the new set-up. Another is that they produced too diverse a range of watches: each model has to sell in mass-production quantities to earn its keep. Foreign import duties made it difficult to sell British watches on continental Europe, and the LWC's business managers may have lacked the necessary financial acumen in an industry which was cut-throat in the extreme. Whatever the reason – or mixture

Pocket watch by the Lancaster
Watch Company of Lancaster,
Pennsylvania, with the movement
visible below

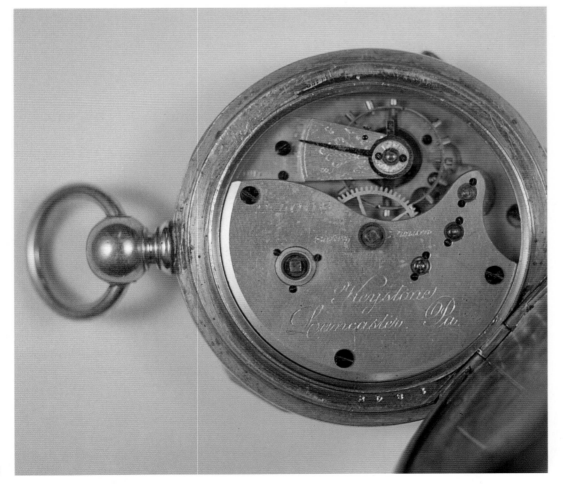

RIGHT
A group of pocket watch
movements arranged around a
Cartier pen watch. The watch in
the lower left-hand corner has
music work – the pin barrel and
comb are clearly visible.

LEFT
A group of lever escapement pocket chronographs which combine timekeeping abilities with a stop-watch function.

RIGHT
Top two rows: eighteenth century pair-cased verge watches. Note extended pendants to accommodate outer case. Third row: Pocket or fob watch by the Swiss watch manufacturer Vacheron & Constantin of Geneva. Bottom row left: Key-wound pocket watch signed by James Murray of London and Melbourne. Right: A half-hunter, which has a glazed aperture in the case through which the time is shown even when the case is closed.

LEFT
Movement of *Waltham* pocket watch. This has a cut bimetallic balance for temperature compensation.

BELOW LEFT
Lever escapement pocket watch by Waltham.

ABOVE RIGHT
Movement of watch by the Elgin National Watch Co of Elgin, Illinois. Engine-turning – or damascening – of the back plates is typical of American watches.

ABOVE FAR RIGHT
Swiss pocket watch by Capt & Freundler of Geneva, c.1790.

BELOW RIGHT
This Elgin pocket watch – like many English watches – carries the retailer's name on the dial.

FAR RIGHT
Movement of Swiss pocket watch.

of reasons – for the failure of the LWC, its demise was a body blow from which British watchmaking was never to recover.

Most of the watch manufacturing machinery used by the Lancashire Watch Company was manufactured in the United States, where the techniques of mass-production in a whole variety of industries were pioneered. It is hardly surprising to find that during the nineteenth century the Americans built up a thriving watch industry of their own, to compete with – if not to rival – the Swiss.

The American watchmaking industry began properly in the middle of the nineteenth century when a trained horologist called Aaron Dennison set up a company with the express purpose of producing watches in large numbers from parts which were interchangeable. The original company – Dennison, Howard and Davis – went through several name changes, eventually building a factory in Waltham, Massachussetts, before being declared bankrupt in 1857 and auctioned off to a group of backers headed by none other than Aaron Dennison. By the end of the decade the company had again been renamed, this time as the American Watch Company, going on to become the American Waltham Watch Company and finally the Waltham Watch Company. This company was

the most prolific of all American watch manufacturers, producing over 30 million pocket watches between its conception in 1850 and its ultimate demise in 1960. Incidentally, Dennison was fired in 1862, and after successfully suing the company for breach of contract went to England where he founded a hugely successful case-making company which remained viable until 1967. Waltham watches found in England today are usually housed in cases made by the Dennison Watch Case Company Ltd.

In the latter years of the nineteenth century Waltham was successfully competing with the Swiss in manufac-

A group of three hunting-cased lever pocket watches. The watch in the bottom left-hand corner is unusual in being key wound from the front and in featuring a 24-hour dial.

turing and selling watches. It had gained a substantial share of the American – and British – markets and now had a number of competitors on the home front, notably Elgin, Hampden and Howard, though none were producing watches in anything like the numbers made by Waltham.

In many ways these early watches were a luxury – and an unnecessary one at that. In the first half of the nineteenth century in particular, people did not keep to the strict timetables that are adhered to today. As railways began to proliferate across America during the second half of the nineteenth century, however, the need for accurate timekeeping and adhering to strict timetables became necessary. This was brought to public attention in the most tragic way when, on 19 April 1891, two trains collided near Kipton, Ohio, killing many on board. The collision was found to be due to the fact that the driver of one of the locomotives had a watch which was showing the wrong time.

This accident had the effect of causing standards of accuracy to be devised covering watches used on the railways – and the 'Railroad watch' was born. Among other things, the standards demanded that Railroad watches had to be accurate to plus or minus 30 seconds per week. Railroad watches were produced in a variety of styles and in great quantities by many American watchmaking companies, including Elgin, Hamilton, Hampden, Illinois and Waltham. Many are still to be found, keeping excellent time, today.

Early American watches were made very much in the

RIGHT
Movement of Elgin pocket watch,
c.1874. This was made for the
cheaper end of the market: most
pivot holes are not jeweled.

BELOW
Swiss watch movement by
Humbert & Ramu. This type of
movement is known as a 'Geneva
bar'. The top plate is replaced by
a series of bars or bridges to
facilitate dismantling and
assembly.

BELOW RIGHT
Front view of Humbert & Ramu
Geneva bar watch.

LEFT
Movement of watch by American
Waltham Watch Company.

BELOW LEFT
Bar movement of watch by James
Nardin of Le Locle, Switzerland.

RIGHT, ABOVE AND BELOW
Engraved rear dust-cover of watch
from the workshops of Sir John
Bennett of Cheapside, an
influential watchmaker in
nineteenth century London who
correctly predicted the demise of
the English watchmaking
industry.

style of the English watches from which they were derived. As the US watchmaking industry grew, however, the watches began to develop characteristics which were more typically American. One particular example was the American trend towards producing cheaper watches. Until the middle of the nineteenth century the watch was an unthinkable – and, as we have seen, largely unnecessary – luxury even for the growing middle classes. This was particularly true of the handmade watches so typical of the English industry. As the use of machinery in America and Switzerland brought the prices of watches down, so the manufacturers began to realize what a vast

137

market existed for cheaper products.

As a result, American watch manufacturers began to produce less expensive watches – still with jeweled wheel trains and escapements – using inferior raw materials. Another line of attack involved producing watches without jewels in either wheel train or escapement, a trend epitomized by the 'Dollar' watch, first introduced by Ingersoll in 1878. This was a watch which was truly within reach of the working man and soon after its introduction Dollar watch fever swept the industry as other manufacturers jumped on the bandwagon. By 1930, some seven million Dollar watches were being produced per annum.

By this time, however, despite these figures, the

LEFT
During the wristwatch boom of the 1980s, Rolex watches became highly collectable, none more so than the distinctive rectangular Rolex Prince shown opposite, bottom row, second from left. Other collectable makes include Patek Philippe, Cartier, Audemars Piguet and Vacheron & Constantin.

RIGHT
Dial of James Nardin watch shown on page 137.

BELOW
Rolex Oyster watches are so called because they are housed in special cases sealed against the ingress of water and have thus found favor among divers. The watch to the extreme right is a Rolex Prince, distinctive because the seconds dial is below the main dial.

Three highly significant wristwatches. Left: *A Harwood –* John Harwood produced one of the first commercially viable self-winding systems. Center: The Hamilton Electric – the American Hamilton Company produced the first electric wristwatches, of highly distinctive appearance. Right: The Bulova Accutron, the first electric wristwatch with the highly accurate tuning-fork escapement.

LEFT AND BELOW
Many wristwatches now are powered by quartz movements, which quickly superseded other electric watches such as the Hamilton and the Bulova Accutron. When quartz watches first appeared, digital time displays were very popular. There has since been a move away from digital in favour of analogue time display.

RIGHT
The Accutron was first produced in 1963. Designed by the Swiss, but put into production by Bulova of the US, the heart of this watch is a tiny tuning fork. The technology on which this watch was based was quickly superseded by quartz.

American watch industry was in terminal decline. The Swiss, later starters in the factory automation process, had finally installed up-to-date machinery which could produce watches by the million. They had also learned modern marketing techniques and were selling aggressively in the United States and Europe. The Swiss companies were also manufacturing and strongly promoting a new style of watch which was worn on the wrist and which had been pioneered by the Swiss firm Girard-Perregaux. Although several American companies were quick off the mark in manufacturing their own wristwatches – Hamilton, Hampden, Waltham and Elgin among them – the glory days of American watchmaking were over.

The origin of the first wristwatch, like so much in horology, is cloaked in obscurity. Watches small enough to have been worn on the wrist exist which are old enough to have verge escapements. That said, true wristwatches were not produced in any numbers before the 1920s when the style began to sweep all before it. In the years which followed, all of the big names in Swiss watchmaking moved large proportions of their production capability over to wristwatch manufacture. Innovations were introduced. Self-winding systems were devised which caused watches to be wound automatically as movements of their wearer's arms turned a rotor inside the body of the watch, the rotor in turn winding up the mainspring. One of the first such systems, the Harwood, was invented by the English watchmaker John Harwood in the early 1920s. A decade or so later Rolex was producing 'automatic' wristwatches using a system which was to become the industry standard. Here the mainspring was wound by rotor movements in either direction and the rotor could swivel through a full 360 degrees.

Other developments included the use of calendar work to display the date through a small aperture in the dial. Watches were subsequently produced with complications such as moonphase indicators, perpetual calendars and even with music work – and throughout the '30s, '40s, '50s and '60s Switzerland was synonymous with the manufacture of reliable and accurate wristwatches.

The first battery-powered wristwatch went into production as early as 1957, manufactured by Hamilton of the United States, and this was quickly followed by models from France, Germany and Switzerland, the most famous of which (before quartz movements became small enough to be incorporated in watches) was probably the Accutron, designed by a Swiss firm but put into production by Bulova of the United States. Here the escapement was replaced by a tuning fork to give greater reliability.

The introduction of quartz technology in the late 1960s threatened the very future of the mechanical wristwatch and by the late '70s and early '80s it seemed to many that days of the latter were strictly numbered. Production figures for mechanical watches went into decline and quartz watches with digital displays became highly fashionable. In more recent years, however, the precision mechanical wristwatch, with analogue display, has returned to popularity, particularly at the top end of the market. Mechanical wristwatches are now selling in numbers again and production figures are rising. Each April, hundreds of new models are introduced at the European Clock, Watch and Jewellery Fair in Basle, Switzerland.

The reasons for this resurgence in popularity of mechanical technology are not at all clear. Perhaps the wearers prefer a watch which does not require a new battery every couple of years. Perhaps they like the fact that the watch is one of the few purely mechanical systems in these days of solid-state electronics. Or perhaps it is just another fashion which will one day bow to the tide of high technology. Only time will tell.

LEFT
Collection of highly distinctive wristwatches from the 1950s and 1960s designed by the French company LIP.

RIGHT
Saratoga: A gents and ladies wristwatch set by Concord of Switzerland.

CHAPTER 12

The Electric Revolution

THREE NAMES crop up with unstinting regularity when discussing the beginnings of electrical horology. The first is that of Matthias Hipp, a Swiss inventor who, in 1834, designed a clock with a pendulum which was impulsed electromagnetically via a 'toggle'. At that time Hipp was only 21 years old, and he did not actually build his electrical clock until 1842, which left him several years behind the other two claimants to the title 'Father of electrical horology'. Nevertheless, Hipp's toggle system went on to become the basis of many later successful electrical clock systems.

The second contender was Carl August Steinheil, a Professor at the University of Munich who, in 1839, patented a mechanism for distributing timekeeping from a central or 'master' clock to a series of subsidiary or 'slave' clock dials. Such master and slave systems were, in subsequent years, greatly improved – particularly by Frank Hope-Jones, of whom more later – and were used throughout the world to distribute time around offices, factories and other large buildings.

The third contender was Alexander Bain, a trained clockmaker from the wilds of Caithness in the far north of Scotland. Though Bain's patent, No. 8783, lagged Steinheil's by a year, the comprehensive nature of the mechanisms described, and the number of truly original developments it anticipates, surely marks the crofter's son out as the true 'father' of electrical horology.

The phenomena of magnetism and static electricity had been known since the Middle Ages. There are records of experiments using naturally occurring magnetic 'lodestone' dating from as early as the thirteenth century. The magnetic compass had been in use aboard ships even earlier than that. And by the end of the sixteenth century English physician William Gilbert had coined the word 'electric' to describe the force of attraction which can be induced in substances such as amber and glass by rubbing them vigorously with a piece of cloth. Elektra, from whom the name was taken, was a goddess in Greek Mythology who was fatally attracted to her father, just as Oedipus was attracted to his mother.

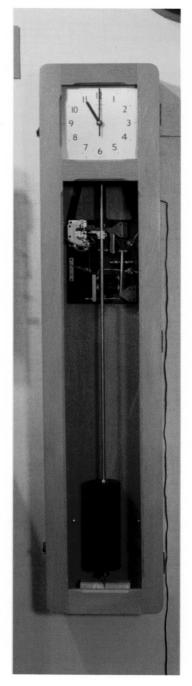

LEFT
A Synchronome master clock and slave dial, c.1955, based on the system invented by Frank Hope-Jones and patented with George Bennett Bowell in 1895.

RIGHT
The Shortt free pendulum clock and, above it, a slave dial. The accuracy of this clock when it was first made amazed the horological world. Its inventor, William Hamilton Shortt, was awarded the Gold Medal of the British Horological Institute in 1932.

It was not until the dying years of the eighteenth century, however, that the existence of 'current' – as opposed to 'static' - electricity was established. In 1791 Luigi Galvani of Bologna University demonstrated that a frog's legs would twitch when subject to an electrical current. At around the same time Count Alessandro Volta, Professor of Physics at Como and Pavia, discovered that the 'new' electricity could be induced by contact between two metals and went on to build the first battery or 'voltaic pile'. In the early years of the nineteenth century research into this new force mushroomed. In England in 1831 Michael Faraday discovered electromagnetic induction and thus laid the foundations not only for the generation of electricity but for a great many of its later applications – including electrical horology.

It was in this fertile and inventive era, when the modern industrial society was being established – that Alexander Bain spent his formative years. Born in 1810, the son of a crofter, Bain was apprenticed to one John Sellar, a watchmaker in Wick. At the age of 19, in 1830, Bain attended a lecture of light, heat, and electricity in nearby Thurso. This was to prove a turning point in his life.

Bain moved to Edinburgh the following year and by 1837 was in London, working as a journeyman clockmaker in Clerkenwell, and attending popular lectures on electricity at the Adelaide Gallery and Polytechnic Institution. By 1838 he had sketched out the design of his first electrical clock and by 1840 had produced rough models of the clock – and of an electrical telegraph, another of his passions.

To take the next step – building and patenting a working clock – needed money which, for a journeyman clockmaker such as Bain, was in rather short supply and when he was apparently offered the patronage of Charles Wheatstone FRS, Professor of Experimental Philosophy at King's College, London, it must have seemed to Bain that the gods were smiling on him. Compared to Bain, Wheatstone was a rich and powerful man who could open doors that Bain could not even knock on. Unfortunately the relationship between the two men soon soured, Bain claiming – with justification – that his erstwhile benefactor had stolen his ideas and was claiming them as his own. The dispute left Bain an embittered man, though in collusion with London clockmaker John Barwise he was still able in October 1840, to apply for the first UK patent covering an electrical clock. That patent was granted in the summer of the following year.

LEFT
The timekeeping of the battery-powered Eureka electric clock was controlled by a huge balance wheel with timing screws round its rim – similar in appearance to the balance wheel of a watch.

RIGHT
Moving magnet master clock by Alexander Bain, the Scottish crofter's son who became the acknowledged father of electrical horology.

LEFT
Movement of the Synchronome
master clocks shown on page
147.

RIGHT
Battery electric Eureka clock
invented by the American T B
Powers in 1908 and produced by
the Eureka Clock Company of
Clerkenwell, London, until the
outbreak of the First World War.

In the years which followed, Bain continued his researches into electrical horology and telegraphy and was granted further patents, one of which was for a clock powered by electricity derived from an 'earth battery', two metal plates buried in soil.

Though the early electrical clocks such as Bain's and Hipp's provided the foundation stone for electrical horology – which, particularly with the emergence of quartz-controlled clocks and watches, has now relegated mechanical horology to a rare craft – early elecrical clocks were not, for the most part, reliable timekeepers. Though a few reliable electrical clocks were made – notably the clock installed at the gate of the Old Observatory, Greenwich, in 1852 by Charles Shepherd, and the Hipp astronomical clock which was shown to have a precision better than the mechanical clocks in the Neuchâtel observatory – they were scorned by makers of conventional mechanical clocks such as Lord Grimthorpe who said that 'anyone who sets to work to invent electric clocks must start with this axiom, that every now and then the electricity will fail to lift anything however small'. Though this statement may seem outrageous today, at the time it was little more than self-evident, and until the beginning of the twentieth century electrical clocks did not appear in numbers in either commercial or domestic environments.

During the latter half of the nineteenth century much research and development work was done into master-and-slave clock systems. People such as R M Lowne and Charles Shepherd in England, Paul Garnier in France, and Warner, Howard and Morse in the United States were all trying to build systems which would be reliable enough – and cheap enough – to be commercially viable. None succeeded, and all through this period of intense development electrical clocks were largely unknown to the common man, unseen outside universities, observatories and the workshops of a few eccentric inventors.

These unreliable clocks used a whole variety of types of mechanism but, according to Frank Hope-Jones the problem lay not in the mechanism for keeping the master clock running, and not in the slave dials, but in the electrical contacts of the master clocks which produced the impulses to actuate the dials. To prove his point, Hope Jones invented what is probably the most successful master clock system of all, the Synchronome, first patented with George Bennett Bowell in 1895.

The Synchronome had several significant advantages over existing master clock systems. Probably the most important of these was that the Synchronome incorporated an automatic rewinding system – not for the first time – which allowed a relatively long interval between contacts. This in turn allowed a firm make and break of contacts and helped to ensure that the pulses were reliable. The Synchronome, mostly due to the reliability of the mechanism and partly, it must be said, due to the promotional abilities of its inventor Hope-Jones, rapidly achieved great popularity as a means of distributing time around offices, factories and other industrial and commercial buildings.

In the years which followed the Synchronome patent, other inventors produced reliable master clock systems: Robert Mann Lowne, in 1901; W E Palmer, watchmaker to

LEFT
Bain's electric master clock of 1885. The pendulum bob of this clock is a magnet.

RIGHT
Movement of the Shortt free pendulum clock showing the synchronizer of the free pendulum.

153

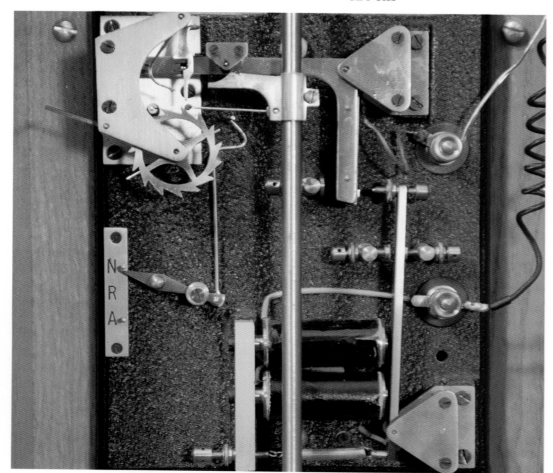

LEFT
Close up of the complex movement of the Shortt free pendulum clock.

RIGHT
The battery-powered Bulle electric clock invented and patented in France by M Favre-Bulle and Professor Marcel Moulon. The pendulum is a hollow solenoid swinging over a magnet with consequent poles.

the South-Eastern and Chatham Railways, in 1902; and notably Isaac Hardy Parsons and Alfred Ernest Joseph Ball who, in 1904, patented the famous Pulsynetic system, later to be manufactured and sold by Gents of Leicester, a name still to found on a great many public clocks today.

Thus 1895 to 1905 saw the development work which led to the widespread acceptance of electricity in time-keeping. Even then, however, there were still no commercially viable electric clocks for domestic households. Mechanical clocks were still being made in increasing numbers to be sold to the ever growing number of households which could now afford what must have appeared an unthinkable luxury in the previous century – their own clock. Over the next 20 years, however, there were two developments which put electrical clocks within reach of the common man.

The first of these was the progress in battery technology to the point where reliability and compactness allowed batteries to be used in domestic appliances. Though Alexander Bain's clocks were powered by batteries – first Daniell cells and then the earth battery – the first battery clock which was a reliable and commercial proposition was the Eureka balance wheel clock, invented by the American Timothy Bernard Powers in 1906 and put into production in a small clock factory in Clerkenwell, London, in 1909. Manufacture continued until the outbreak of war in 1914 by which time approximately 10,000 of these clocks had been made.

Early Eureka clocks had visible movements mounted on a base which concealed the battery and covered by a glass dome to protect them from dust. The giant slow-moving balance wheel – very similar in appearance to the balance wheel of a watch – was a very attractive feature and the manufacurers made good use of its hypnotic effect. Strangely, perhaps, later models were housed in a variety of case style, some of which concealed the movement entirely.

Other battery-driven electrical clocks followed the Eureka, the most popular of which by far was the Bulle clock, originally patented in France by M Favre-Bulle and Professor Marcel Moulon. This was a pendulum-controlled clock in which the pendulum is a hollow solenoid swinging from side to side over a magnet with 'consequent' poles – south at each end and north in the middle. Like the Eureka, early Bulle clocks were housed in cases made largely of glass, allowing the motion of the pendulum to be seen. Later models appeared in a great variety of case styles, many of which hid the movement from view entirely. Though the movements of these clocks were manufactured in France, many of the later models were assembled in England by a company known as Bulle Products Ltd of London, the company's English subsidiary. The Bulle clock was produced in even greater numbers than the Eureka, production continuing until the outbreak of the Second World War.

The second development which was responsible for

LEFT
Bulle clock with electrically
maintained Hipp-type pendulum.

ABOVE RIGHT
Pair of synchronous electric clocks
which were in common usage by
the 1960s.

RIGHT
A fine example of a Bulle clock
dating from the early years of the
twentieth century made by the
Eureka Clock Co., London.

the appearance of electric clocks in a large number of domestic households – larger by far than battery clocks like the Bulle and Eureka – was the invention of the mains electric 'synchronous' motor, which used the effect of alternating current to make the motor revolve. The development of nationally synchronized power supplies obviously helped and, exemplified in the UK by the setting up of the Central Electricity Generating board in 1927 and the establishment in the year which followed of the 'National Grid', a national network which distributed mains electric power to homes and factories throughout the country alternating at a uniform 50 cycles per second (now know as 50 Hertz).

The idea behind the synchronous clock was first patented in 1916 by the American Henry Warren, and the first synchronous clocks were marketed by the Warren Clock Company under the name 'Telechron'. These reliable little clocks can easily be distinguished from battery clocks like the Bulle and the Eureka by the fact that they are plugged into the mains electricity supply. In Britain the first synchronous clocks were manufactured by Everett Edgecumbe & Co. A great many other companies subsequently produced synchronous electric clocks, by the million, in a wide variety of case styles, and this type of clock remained popular as domestic timekeepers until the 1960s, when they were gradually replaced by reliable and cheaply produced battery clocks with quartz controlled movements. Synchronous clocks, among the most accurate domestic timekeepers ever made, can still be seen today, particularly on electric cookers. Their fatal drawback was that they needed to be plugged into the mains: they thus lacked portability and were at the mercy of unreliable electricity supplies.

INDEX